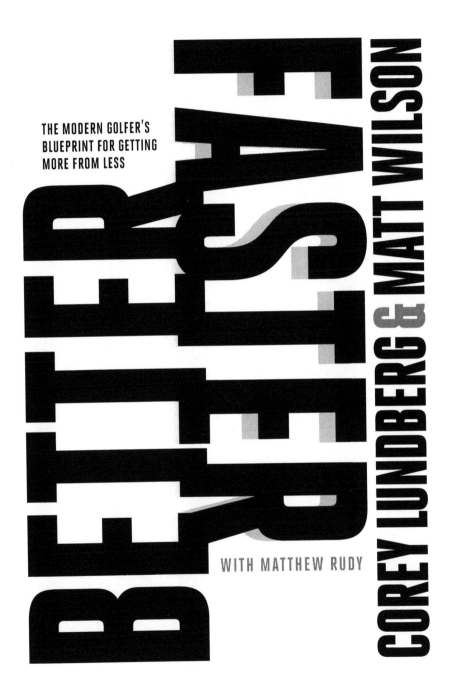

FASTER

BETTER

THE MODERN GOLFER'S
BLUEPRINT FOR GETTING
MORE FROM LESS

WITH MATTHEW RUDY

COREY LUNDBERG & MATT WILSON

Printed in the United States of America

First Printing, 2017

ISBN-13: 978-1545286425
ISBN-10: 1545286426

Designed by Tim Oliver (timothypoliver.com)

*To our students, who continually strive
to be better than they were yesterday, and for whom
the game means so much. We strive to equal or exceed
your efforts in the pursuit of your personal best.*

CONTENTS

FOREWORD BY CAMERON McCORMICK

YOU CAN FIND GOLF INSTRUCTORS all over the world, but the fishbowl we're all in is actually pretty small. If you're passionate about learning, you'll tend to run into people who are on the same mission.

That's how it happened with Corey Lundberg and Matt Wilson. I first met Matt when he called and asked if he could come and shadow me during my own teaching. He came down once a month for eight months, and we got to know each other well. Corey I knew from his work at a neighboring club, and I could see he and Matt had that same passion.

Together, they've been exploring what I think is an incredibly important part of the learning landscape. There's plenty of research out there, plenty of theories and plenty of "methods." But how do you sort through that information and use it to help build better golfers? It isn't about proving how much science you unload in a 50-minute practice session. Corey and Matt are driven to understand the science of learning and combine that knowledge with the practical experience of coaching players at every level.

For sure we're all cut from the same cloth. We're looking to conquer the unknowns, and find solutions that will work when the round—and the tournament—is on the line.

Now, I'm fortunate to partner with Corey in Dallas, at Altus Performance, and Matt is doing great things with his students in Canada and California. If you don't know about them, you will—and *Better, Faster* is the perfect introduction. It has ideas you can incorporate into your practice routine immediately, and you'll finally start seeing some carryover from what you learn how to do and what you actually do when you play.

Cameron McCormick
Altus Performance
2015 PGA Teacher of the Year
Member of *Golf Digest's 50 Best Teachers* list
Dallas, TX

FOREWORD BY DR. TIM LEE

MOST OF WHAT WE KNOW about motor learning—the way the human mind acquires new skills—has come in the last 35 or 40 years, thanks to some fascinating research by scientists around the word. I spent my university career immersed in that same research—and publishing some of my own—and it has been amazing to see the impact on disciplines ranging from sports to elementary education. We're now in an era where we can see exactly which parts of the learning experience are useful for the teacher and the student, and which parts are actually getting in the way of skill acquisition. That's a big deal, with big ramifications in human performance.

Since my retirement from teaching at McMaster University, I've had more time to enjoy one of my favorite activities—playing golf. It might sound funny coming from a motor learning researcher, but I've been a self-taught player my whole golf career. I've always been interested to read and watch the latest methods instructors use to teach what is one of the most complicated motor movements an athlete can try to do. I was always curious to see when instructors would catch on to the great information coming out of motor learning research.

When I stumbled onto **CuriousCoaches.com**, I found two instructors who have done just that.

Corey Lundberg and Matt Wilson understand that the ways most players practice and play is fundamentally different. Hitting balls mindlessly doesn't help you play better golf. The game itself has endless variety, different conditions and different emotions. It's fundamentally more difficult than hitting shots with no consequences in the controlled environment of a practice range. The way you get better faster is to create practice scenarios that build basic skills and then seek to replicate what you would experience on the course.

Better, Faster shows you how.

I speak the language of a scientist. That has its place, but what Corey and Matt have been able to do is take the most advanced research in motor learning and translate it into real concrete practice plans spoken in the language of the golfer. They will show you how to acquire real, measurable skills that translate to the course.

Dr. Tim Lee
Professor Emeritus in Kinesiology
McMaster University
Hamilton, Ontario, Canada

INTRODUCTION

WHO ARE WE, AND WHY ARE YOU HERE?

T'S THE CONSTANT STRUGGLE. No matter what your handicap is, you've had a round—or even a month—when you hit lots of good shots and turn in a good score.

But there's always what the data scientists call "regression to the mean."

Those scores go back to where they usually are, and you play pretty much like the player you've always been.

Why does the game seem so resistant to consistent, long-term improvement?

Why are so many players playing the same game they did five, ten or 20 years before?

And why is this true in a time when there's more access to great information, informed teaching and fantastic technology than ever before?

Players and coaches have more information than ever, but there's still a gap between what players know they're "supposed" to do and what they actually execute on the course.

The nuts and bolts of how a player should actually swing the club is obviously important to know. If you don't move the club and your body in a coordinated, repeatable way, you aren't going to make any progress. You need a functional base of technique in each of the game's skill areas to shoot scores at a given level.

But there's also a second part of that learning equation that's equally important. It's the application of the information you get about *how* to make more coordinated, repeatable swings—combined with an ability to adapt that functional technique to all the different situations you will encounter on the course.

You need to have the right information, the right plan to *apply* the information, and then go do the work in a way that matches how your brain actually receives and processes information and how the body can adapt to a variety of conditions.

The information has to be useful, and you have to be able to access it when you need it.

Otherwise, it's no help.

From the time we were beginning teachers, our goal has been to bridge that gap. There's plenty of information—great information—out there, but we wanted to both teach our players what to do and coach them on how completely integrate the new information into their game so that it could show up on the scorecard.

For Matt, it started after he graduated from Long Island University, where he was captain of the golf team. He went home to Toronto and worked under *Golf Magazine* Top 100 Teacher Henry Brunton for more than three years, and helped Henry open his academy at Eagles Nest. From there, Matt moved to La Rinconada Country Club, in Los Gatos, Calif., where he built one of the most successful junior development programs on the West Coast. Now, as Director of Next Generation Performance for Golf Canada, Matt is responsible for identifying and developing Canada's next wave of international competitors and coaches.

Corey graduated from Arizona State's professional golf management program and moved to the Club at Carlton Woods, outside Houston, where his adult and junior coaching programs were some of the most sought after in the area. In the summer of 2016, Corey relocated to Dallas to partner with Cameron Mc-Cormick to launch Altus Performance—an elite coaching organization based at the new Trinity Forest Golf Club.

From the beginning, we were circulating in the same training programs. Matt worked for Henry Brunton, and Corey was one of the first coaches to go through Henry's certification program. Both of us spent long hours in the car driving to watch Cameron and Tour short game instructor James Sieckmann work with elite players.

By 2013, Cameron knew we had the same values and the same teaching philosophy, so he introduced us. We discovered we were reading the same books, immersed in the same research, and had the same interests. Corey started CuriousCoaches.com, a popular blog about the science and art of teaching, but as his real-life coaching business was expanding, he didn't have as much time to keep it updated. So Matt joined in, and we've been working together to both improve our coaching skills and share best practices with other teachers and players.

In the last 10 years, the variety of academic research on peak performance has exploded, and we've spent hundreds of hours combing this material looking for elements that could translate into a practical teaching approach. That means asking critical questions: Something worked in a controlled experiment, but how does it translate onto the teaching tee?

From mentors like Cameron, Henry and James, we learned very quickly that the scientific principles of motor learning are important, but they aren't the only tools necessary for this kind of work. Both of us had the same experience a lot of coaches

go through at the beginning of their careers. A student would come with a common problem—say, a slice—and we'd give them the "fix" we had learned by watching a thousand lessons.

Change the grip.

Change the ball position.

Change the face.

And so on. And so on.

That student would hit some shots and see some real improvement, and leave happy. The next student would come with a similar problem, and we'd apply the same solutions. But the results would be totally different.

The "fixes" wouldn't work at all.

And then the first player—who left happy—would come back in three weeks and complain that the "fix" had worn off, and he was back where he started. Or he would tell us that he could feel what he was supposed to do when he was hitting practice balls, but that it left him on the course, when it counted.

This is the fundamental grind most players experience—the cycle of trying to improve, getting a bit better, then regressing—that a lot of coaching fails to solve. It was happening to us, and it was getting very frustrating. Standing there with players in a "golf classroom"—the practice range—and giving prescriptive fixes in an environment disconnected from where the actual scoring happens wasn't producing consistent, repeatable results.

But, as you'll read in the next chapter, we were lucky to find some resources that pointed to a different way—a different way to coach, and a different way for students to learn.

It mixes the science of skill acquisition—how people actually learn—with the art of coaching. The validation of that

approach came from seeing first-hand top coaches use it with with the best players in the game. Cameron did it with Masters Champion Jordan Spieth and a stable of highly-ranked junior, collegiate and tour players. James Sieckmann has had the same success with variety of players on all the major tours. Seeing that success showed us that there was another way.

All you have to do is look at the work Cameron has done with Jordan to see a prime example—and a prime template—of how we strive to combine technical improvements with skill development. Jordan's swing matches who he is and what his body wants to do—and he plays with an incredibly high level of skill and tactical intelligence. His mindset is perfect for high performance, and he consistently plays his best golf when the stakes are highest.

The results speak for themselves. Jordan was on the leaderboard at the Byron Nelson when he was 16 years old, and quickly mastered every level of competition. At Texas, he won three tournaments and helped the Longhorns win the NCAA team title as a freshman. After turning pro, he won his way into full status on the PGA Tour as a 20-year-old at the John Deere Classic. In 2014, he almost won his first major, at the Masters, where he would have been the youngest green jacket winner ever. Learning from that experience, he dominated the 2015 Masters from start to finish, then followed it up with another clutch performance at the U.S. Open. With him along the way for each of these accomplishments was his coach, Cameron—always emphasizing skill over style and helping his student adapt his skills to each level of competition.

Every player on the range at a PGA Tour event has incredible skills.

But what Jordan has been able to do is translate those skills into scores under pressure, and he's done it more quickly than almost any other player.

The stakes might be different for you, but the overall goal is the same.

It isn't about watching somebody demonstrate the perfect motion and trying to copy it over and over again. It's about identifying the most important skills, developing them in the right environment and then translating them to the course quickly and efficiently.

It's about getting better, faster.

• • •

Sounds great, right?

OK, so how do we do that?

In this book, we're going to give you an operating system for your own skill development in three critical areas of the game—ball-striking, putting and wedge play. We'll show you the building blocks you need to maximize your skills in each area, and give you a specific game plan to knit those skills into on-course performance. We will also deliver those training plans in a way that is interactive and responsive to your unique needs as a player—whether that's an improvement to your technique, diversifying skills so you can adapt to different situations, or just building some confidence.

What makes this different than other golf instruction plans?

We're going to help you develop those skill sets while working within the time constraints of normal people with regular jobs and outside lives. Jordan Spieth and Rory McIlroy dedicate thousands of hours per year toward practice, training and competing, because that is their profession.

Here, you're going to learn how to incorporate the same skill development techniques those players use to achieve your own peak performance.

Does that mean you'll be able to practice for 30 minutes a month and break par by the end of the summer? Not exactly. But you'll learn how to practice efficiently and actually get measurable on-course improvement from the practicing you do.

It will take time, but we can help it take less of it.

In the first chapter, we're going to identify the main problem—you practice, but you don't get any better—and explain why it's happening. Next, we'll take a brief tour around the world of peak performance, and talk about some of the leading research and coaching techniques that are changing the way players train and improve. In the third chapter, we'll take you through a simple (but comprehensive) self-assessment survey that will clearly identify the areas of your game that need the most attention—and which learner needs your customized training plan should address. This survey will become your go-to tool as you systematically improve your game piece by piece. Next, we'll lay out the practice programs for each game area—ball-striking, putting and wedge play—and give you concrete steps to make your way through the improvement plan. To finish, we'll talk about the future and how to build this experience into a repeatable system, and then leave you with our favorite resources you can access for more information.

It's time to play.

CHAPTER 1

THE PROBLEM: YOU PRACTICE, BUT AREN'T GETTING ANY BETTER

IF YOU BOUGHT THIS BOOK, desire isn't a problem for you. You want to get better. You're willing to practice. You're willing to invest whatever spare time you have in your game to shoot lower scores.

But you're probably also coming to this book frustrated by your progress (or lack of it).

Maybe you've played for a long time, but you've stalled at a certain handicap. Or you're a beginner who is intimidated by what can be a pretty steep learning curve. Or you're a junior player who has put in tons of time both with a coach and on your own, but you haven't been able to take that important step over to shooting rounds consistently below par.

Interestingly enough, every kind of player—the ones we just described, and any others you can think of—have different kinds of strengths and weaknesses, different bodies and different approaches, but they're all the same in one important way.

They're all human.

Our brains are all wired to process information in a very specific way. And if you're bumping into that frustration that is a natural part of learning any skill, it's actually a good sign.

You can't develop a new skill without encountering some failure on the way. Failure actually means you're operating at the brink of your ability as you stretch to new heights. Without that challenge, you don't learn. But without the right mindset for learning—or the right practice framework—you aren't going to improve at your peak rate, no matter how much effort and good intention you put into it. And you run a high risk of actually stalling out and getting worse.

What do we mean?

Think about your car. Let's say the engine starts making some funny noises, and you notice a puddle of oil on the floor of the garage.

You're determined to fix the car, so you crank it up on a jack, and you disconnect the first part you see underneath—the oil filter. You go buy a new filter, and screw it on. But when you drive the car, it still makes the same noises. So you jack it up again and try something different. This time, you disconnect the mufflers, to see what happens.

Now, when the car drives, it still leaks oil and it still makes the original sound, but it makes a whole new set of bad sounds from the muffler being disconnected.

You could keep taking things off and putting them on again in different combinations, hoping to luck into either the real solution or a combination of faults that cover up the problem temporarily.

Or, you could diagnose the problem correctly, identify the real solution, and go about executing your more thoughtful plan for a long-term repair.

Golf isn't any different.

The vast majority of players are searching. They're looking

for an idea or a drill that will prove to be the single magic bullet—the one that will produce that consistent, high, straight ball flight everybody wants.

And since we've all hit a perfect shot or two, we know what it feels like—and we're chasing to get it back again.

So you're on the range, searching, and you're willing to try just about anything you hear (or read). And maybe what you're trying provides a nice Band-Aid for your game, and you hit a few good shots.

But as soon as that thing you're trying doesn't work, what do you do? You ditch it and try something else.

The cycle repeats itself over and over. And you're in the same situation as the person trying to fix that car. Instead of examining the system, finding the constants and trying single variables, you've built a system where everything is a variable.

You've seen it in action, in your own game.

Maybe you read a tip in one of the golf magazines about hitting your driver better. You're headed out to play on Saturday, so you get a bucket of balls beforehand and try the new thing—let's use a common Band-Aid for an example, say, pausing at the top of your backswing.

After 10 or 15 balls, you start to get the feel for it, and you hit some good ones. Now, you go to the first tee and try it. It doesn't work as well, and you make a swing you self-diagnose as 'too quick'. The ball goes low and left, into the trees. You try again on the third hole, and you get the same bad result.

By the fifth hole, you've decided to ditch the pause, and go back to what you were doing before. You're convinced the tip was junk.

Was it?

Not necessarily. We're big fans of what most magazines and instruction websites try to do. If the goal is to make players better, we support that.

And that specific tip about pausing at the top might have been a great one for you and your swing. But because you incorporated it into your swing the wrong way (and, really, not at all), it didn't have much of a chance as sticking.

Let's go back to fixing cars for a second. There are hundreds of different parts coordinating simultaneously to make the car run. The golf swing is similar. Many of those swing parts work on their own, because they've been automated by years of moving in the same way. It's no different than how you drive to work every morning. The route has pretty much become automated.

But those parts of your swing that are typically 'well-oiled' and ingrained get disrupted when you place all of your attention on one single piece of the swing. We'll talk more about this later, but that type of internal focus of attention is rarely a recipe for enhanced performance on the actual course.

Because your Band-Aid tip didn't work right away, it got tossed out—one of a dozen that are probably always coming and going in your game.

Because you're not evaluating the tip—or your game—the right way, you're going to have a heck of time finding things that truly work. And even when you find something that could be great, you toss it before you have a chance to truly get it in place.

All of that might sound frustrating—and maybe even hopeless.

After all, if a good tip doesn't help, what will?

Our goal here is to help give you context to your swing, and to the ways you're trying to make it better.

Instead of randomly adding and subtracting new parts (new ideas), you'll get a better idea of how to pick parts, and understand the two very distinct pieces of the "mastery" process.

When you jump from tip to tip and toss things out as quickly as they come in, you're never increasing your level of mastery.

In other words, you're going to surf along at roughly the same talent/skill/athleticism plateau where you currently play. You might do some things differently, but it doesn't mean that the overall result will be better performance.

Or, you might be determined enough to work on a new skill to the point where you start to see and feel some of it in your swing. But having that skill be durable and adaptable enough to make it to the course in tact—and to make it through a pressure situation out on the course—are different levels of "mastery," and ones most players never learn how to access.

You will now.

If all of this sounds new and challenging, you're not alone. Even the best players in the world experience similar frustrations as they go through the process of improving their games. And they're playing in an arena where fractions of strokes on average over the course of the season mean the difference between winning tournaments and losing their playing status.

We started working with a professional rookie this season who came to us after a season of poor performances. He was looking for some new answers. His hopes and expectations were exactly the same as those of most of our recreational clients when they come in for the first time.

He wanted us to watch him hit balls and identify the technical deficiency in his swing that was holding him back.

After a thorough assessment of his skills and technique, we explained to him that his golf swing was highly functional. It produced a level of ball control that got him through the junior golf ranks to a scholarship at a top school, and it now gave him the chance to make a living playing golf.

Our biggest job was not fixing his swing—which was clearly good enough to shoot low scores.

It was to shift his mindset so that he could see that there might be another way to go about improving.

So our first action was to create a practice plan that addressed his unique needs as a player. There were some technical adjustments he could make, but more than anything, we wanted to diversify his technique so he felt like he owned his swing—and could transfer his skills to whatever shot he needed to hit.

He came for a traditional lesson, and left with a comprehensive performance plan. It laid out the technical keys we identified as important, but more importantly, it emphasized the specific steps he needed to take to diversify those skills. (You're getting an adapted form of that process in the pages of this book).

After he spent some time with this plan, the player came back to us for a follow up. He was happy to report that his scores were going down—but the most interesting byproduct of his work was that he was having way more fun both practicing and competing.

Instead of grinding it out on the range in the endless search for perfect technique, he was attacking skill development in a way that made him enjoy the experience of chasing his goals.

He was getting better fast, and enjoying the process.

And don't think this type of experience is limited to great players. There's no doubt that having a high level of technical skill gives you the luxury of focusing mostly on layering these skill elements—instead of, say, fighting through a grip change or a dramatic adjustment in club delivery. But the same focused, organized approach to improving your base level of technique can be done in a way that lines up with how people best learn new skills.

You're going to hear us say this over and over again in this book.

You're not as broken as you think.

And good golf is closer than it appears. It doesn't always require more practice. Just better within the time you're currently committing.

Need more proof?

Let's compare two different range sessions. The first scenario happens every day on ranges around the world. The second is one performed by one of Matt's top junior players.

The first player comes to the range with his full bag and a large bucket of balls. Without any warm up, the driver is the first club to come out of the bag. He gets right to it with full speed driver swings. The first few are near grounders but eventually he finds something of a rhythm and we are able to assess the overall pattern and ball flight tendencies.

He makes a pretty athletic move, but his swing is somewhat steep and comes from over the top—something many, many players fight.

After about a dozen balls, he makes a couple of slower speed pantomimed half-downswings, moving the club in a

more outward path in hopes to solve for the right miss.

You can almost see the gears in his head turning, and the thought bubble popping up above.

Don't come over the top. Hit it from the inside.

At real speed, that attempted inside move causes him to hang back on and completely stall any attempts at a pivot through impact. Even though his path has improved, he's still trapped in the fundamental problem he started with. The old path was just a response to an outrageously open face, and now with his new path, he either hits massive block cuts or flips the face hard and late to produce a handful of hard, low hooks.

After that, he goes back to what he was doing before and hits a few more steep, high fades. Looking out at the markers downrange, he turns his feet as if to aim more at one of the markers to the left. But after hitting another half dozen balls, his stance drifted back over to being square with the leading edge of the turf mat. Most of his balls peeled of the same way—weak and to the right.

In comparison, our players come to the course with a totally different mindset and approach to their practice time. The first thing you would notice when comparing these sessions is the sense of purpose. We don't all have the luxury of devoting hours to our golf obsession. Many golfers are constrained by a lack of time and a litany of real-world obligations. So it stands to reason that a more focused, purposeful approach would be more effective than the aimless strategy deployed in the first example.

And the other difference you'll notice is that our players have task-based plans rather than time-based ones. Where the first player decided he was going to hit balls for an hour,

our player comes to the practice facility with a job to do. He has a list of tasks we've prescribed, and once he's done, he's done. It might take 30 minutes one day and 90 another day. Regardless, he leaves the range with the peace of mind that comes with knowing he has made progress toward his goals.

And that may be the biggest shift in mindset—knowing you've made progress, vs. guessing.

The first golfer may have thought he worked on his game, but really he just got some exercise—and maybe some mental gymnastics trying to work out his fix for the day. Our player leaves with a sense of accomplishment and specific measures on how he performed and where he needs to improve.

Here's an example plan for one of our players:

TEAM ALTUS 8-WEEK
TRAINING PROGRAM

Designed for:
Training Timeframe:

TRAINING PROGRAM OVERVIEW	TASK DESCRIPTION

TASK DESCRIPTION

For the next 8 weeks, we will be placing emphasis on the following key performance indicators. Closing these critical performance gaps represent an opportunity to quickly impact scores. Start each practice session in a blocked practice setting-- focusing on any recommended form changes. Then move on to the training tasks included here.

Listed below are your current stats in these areas along with goals for the next 8 week period. Allow these objectives to provide purpose to your training. A well-designed program leaves no doubt that progress will be made. Work the plan diligently and we will review the stats in 8 weeks to see the direct impact of your efforts.

TECHNICAL NOTES
Complete your blocked tasks as prescribed by Matt and Corey prior to diving into this menu of skill development tasks.

TRIDENT
The goal is to expand on your ability to create a predictable curve by attempting to produce a variety of curves. Start by hitting a cut shot to your target by shifting the direction your club is traveling through impact to match up with the leftward pointing rod while pointing the face between the inside rod and target line rod at impact. Next try to draw it at your target-- shift the directing your club is traveling through impact to match up with the rightward pointing rod while pointing the face between the inside rod and target line rod at impact.

CONTRA
Hit the following 11 shots to the same target in the specified order (P.S.: This refers to the famous cheat code to the leg- endary Nintendo game, Contra!!): High Shot, High Shot, Low Shot, Low Shot, Curve Le , Curve Right, Curve Le , Curve Right, One club less (swing hard), One club more (swing so), Stock shot. COMPLETION CUE: If you're able to have more than 60% of your shots finish inside the radius, you are performing at a high level.

DRIVER CURVE CONE
Place an alignment rod down the target line in front of your ball. Place a second rod to the left of the first rod, angled 20 or so degrees left of the target— place a 3rd rod on the opposite side. The goal is to start your drives inside the 'cone' and keep them from curving outside of it. Hit 5 successful draws that start inside the right cone, but don't cross the target line-- repeat with 5 fades. Then do the same with a secondary driving club. Log the number of balls required to complete.

PRIMARY GOAL
BIRDIE OPPORTUNITY %
CURRENT   GOAL
30% ➡ 40%

SUPPORTING GOAL
FAIRWAY %
CURRENT   GOAL
48% ➡ 60%

RAT RACE
Design: Place 10 balls around the hole at random distances from four to 12 feet from the hole.
Objective: Select a putt to start from. The goal is to make it around, holing out all 10 balls. Make the rst putt to advance to the next location. If you miss a putt three times in a row, move back to the previous location.
Completion Cue: You've completed the task when you have made it to the nal location and holed out from there. This is a great game to play against an opponent in a race to be the rst to hole out from all 10 locations.

SECONDARY GOAL
STROKES GAINED PUTTING
CURRENT   GOAL
-0.9 ➡ 0

PAR, BIRDIE, BOGEY PUTTING
Tools: Putter, nine balls (three marked "+1," three marked "0" and three marked "-1" in sharpie
Design: Pick a hole and toss up the balls to randomly distribute them between three and 15 feet from the hole. Working your way from farthest to closest to the hole, putt all nine putts keeping track of your score. Balls marked with +1 are for bogey, balls marked with -1 are for birdie, and balls marked with 0 are for par.
Objective: Your goal is to score as low as possible. Compete against others or against your personal best to nish with the lowest score.

Which kind of player do you want to be?

CHAPTER 2

THE REASONS: A BRIEF TOUR AROUND THE WORLD OF PEAK PERFOMANCE

I THINK WE CAN ALL AGREE that golf is complicated. It's more than just a series of physical movements to improve. You're dealing with strategic decisions, changing conditions and managing your emotions, among other things.

So it shouldn't be a surprise that a lot of players have common issues with their games—and a lot of those problems have been persistent ones for them over a lot of years.

It's a hard game to learn, and it's a hard game to master.

Of course, that's part of what attracts a lot of people to it. But it also creates a ton of frustration—and sends a lot of people out of the game.

From the very beginning of our careers as teachers and coaches, we've been looking for ways to use the most up-to-the-minute research in human performance and motor learning to make the road to improvement more understandable, more relatable, more manageable—and, most importantly, shorter.

Ben Hogan deserves a tremendous amount of respect for "digging it out of the dirt," and figuring out his game for himself. Almost 70 years later, we're fortunate to have the work of top scientists, researchers and coaches that reveals a more direct path to "skill acquisition," improved performance and increased enjoyment.

In this chapter, we're going to talk about some of the research science that has been most influential in our teaching—and how we've adapted that information to work inside the world of golf instruction and coaching. It's obviously important to get the right mechanical fundamentals when you're working on your swing, but it's just as important (if not more so) to receive those fundamentals in a way you can most efficiently process and incorporate them. In other words, HOW you learn and practice is just as important as WHAT you're learning and practicing. As you'll see, the 'how' plays a major role in determining the degree to which you'll reproduce your performance in practice, on the course.

Like we said in the introduction, there is no shortage of information out there. With an iPad and an Internet connection, you can watch virtually any famous swing since Bobby Jones, in slow motion and from a bunch of different angles. You can see thousands of golf lessons.

But if you don't understand how your brain best receives information, and how to scale your learning to add skills on top of other skills, your golf game will look like club hoarder's garage. It'll be filled with stuff, but with no practical way to get to it or use it all.

We were learning from our mentors the best ways to teach and coach players. We wanted to add to that knowledge some of the best practices identified and examined by researchers who were interested in the science of learning and performance. We dove deep into the process of understanding more about how the brain best learns and what we need to do

to better facilitate the storage and retrieval of information—
not how to hit a fade or draw. Hundreds of books, dozens of
seminars and plenty of late night conversations later—we
identified three major areas of study and innovation that we
committed to making a part of our teaching and coaching
strategies going forward:

→ DELIBERATE PRACTICE

→ REPRESENTATIVE LEARNING

→ FINDING YOUR CHALLENGE POINT

For the last five years, our job has been to figure out the
best way to integrate those ideas into day-to-day golf instruction, player coaching and program building at our facilities. If
you've followed us on our blog, **CuriousCoaches.com**, you've
seen some of that journey. What you're reading about here is
the result of this research and thousands of hours of refine-
ment on the practice tee with golfers at every level—from be-
ginners to college players to PGA Tour players.

While it sounds complicated and academic, it is a blueprint
or framework you can use to essentially hack—or accelerate—
the learning process.

Let's talk a little bit more about each of these areas—which
will give you a preview of the practice programs that will be
coming in the next chapters.

DELIBERATE PRACTICE

OUR FIRST EXPOSURE to the world of peak performance outside of golf came from reading some research papers that might be familiar. Malcolm Gladwell's book Outliers famously outlined Dr. Anders Erickson's concept of skill acquisition—that it takes 10,000 hours of deliberate practice to become an expert. After reading Dr. Erickson's original research paper on the subject, and seeking out other perspectives in the world of academia, we saw that Gladwell's version of the 10,000-hour concept was an oversimplification of the development of skill. First, practice time and improvement don't necessarily work in a 1:1 ratio—no matter how "deliberate." The amount of time you put in doesn't correlate to a specific output of "improvement." Time is certainly correlated to improvement and gaining expertise, but it isn't the *cause* of it.

Other qualitative factors underpin the developmental process—character-based things like grit, determination and desire, and structure-based things like we're going to talk about in this book. How relevant the training is to your needs and how well it's built obviously are big influencers in an outcome. And, unlike what the 10,000-hour rule suggests, learning isn't a linear progression. It's a long process that has streaks and slumps, while trending upward over time.

The main takeaway for us was not the number of hours it would take to go from two-year-old Tiger Woods hitting balls on the Mike Douglas Show to winning the Masters in 1997. It was that *deliberate practice* is a fundamental part of improvement, and that we needed to understand what "deliberate" really means when it comes to learning—and mastering—a skill.

So, what separates deliberate practice from "standard" practice?

Here's a common scenario. You go to the putting green and drop three balls. For 20 minutes, you roll some putts to different targets around the green, without really keeping track of your results. At the end of it, you feel like you got some work in, and that your "feel" improved. You've "practiced."

But think about it.

What did you really accomplish?

Even though it seems like you practiced, what you've really done is spend time putting. Deliberate practice is fundamentally different. First, deliberate practice is objective-driven. You're pursuing a general goal in each session, and the achievement of that goal is supported through completing specific tasks that are directly related to successful performance. In other words, everything you do is rooted in, and in alignment with, your improvement.

For example, Tiger Woods often practices hitting putts swinging the putterhead through a very narrow gate of tees. He's working on the specific skills of hitting putts in the center of the face, and of starting the ball on the exact intended start line. Both of these skills correlate positively to controlling speed and holing putts. After he completes a pre-determined number of successful repetitions, he knows his actions and training moved the performance needle.

You need a general goal and tasks that work toward that goal. But without a system of regular feedback, you won't know if you're achieving your goals. Think back to kindergarten. When you were learning addition, you'd get a big red X on your paper

when you wrote down the wrong answer to 2+2. When you got it right, you got a green check mark or a smiley face.

Those marks were the feedback sources that guided us on the path to learning addition. Learning golf is no different. You need the X or check within the context of your regular practice. Unless you have it, you won't know if you're moving forward or backward.

Where does that feedback come from? The senses—sight, hearing, and touch—all provide feedback. In Tiger's putting drill, seeing the putterhead either move through the tee gate or run into it gives instant feedback. If you're working with a coach, he or she watches what you're doing and gives commentary that you're hearing. Feedback gives the learner information he or she uses to either repeat or modify the execution of a given skill.

Why is deliberate practice so important?

Because people are amazing. They can learn anything—even the wrong thing. So if you're practicing without direction, you probably aren't improving—and if you're directed in your practice to the wrong thing, you're getting a lot better at executing the wrong action.

Our goal in every lesson—and in this book—is to give you a system of deliberate practice, and to give you evidence of correctness. We want you to learn what you want and need to learn—not reinforce negative patterns and non-functional skills.

If you're doing it right, you're using your practice time for directed improvement, and you're scaling up your practice over time to become more and more difficult. It's no different than going to the gym. If you're trying to build muscle, you increase the weight you lift over time, which is harder to do, until you become stronger.

Dr. Erickson's research was the jumping off point for both Gladwell's 10,000-hours chapter, and for Daniel Coyle's *The Talent Code*, where he traveled around the world to investigate places that were producing talent in numbers out of proportion to their size. He found that expert performance—whether it was in academics, music, sports or any other acquired skill—doesn't come from inherent physical or mental advantages. It comes from understanding and exploiting the human brain's learning mechanisms and how the body responds and adapts to training.

In other words, anybody can get better, faster. That said, deliberate (or more "engaged") practice isn't the be all end all. There's more to it. Persistence needs motivation. This, in our view, is the key ingredient to sustained growth; a strong fire that burns within. Practice, therefore, has to come with a piece that increases the strength of the fire that burns inside you. What does that mean? It needs to be something you WANT to do; it needs to be enjoyable, not drudgery.

REPRESENTATIVE LEARNING

THROUGHOUT OUR LEARNING AND RESEARCH PROCESS, we would pick through different research papers and identify operating theories that would make for good experimentation inside the world of golf instruction. We wanted to figure out what was applicable and relevant.

We'd parse out some of the terminology in the papers, then both of us would record ourselves on video trying to explain what the terms meant and how it was "actionable." We were in pursuit of knowledge and information that we could put into play. We'd ship the videos back and forth from Texas to California, and ask each other questions about the definitions. We did this with more than 40 journal articles and research papers.

One of our favorites was a (relatively) less-known paper by Dr. Ian Renshaw, a researcher from the Queensland University of Technology, in Australia, about building internal motivation for practice among athletes.

One of the key concepts in this paper—nonlinear pedagogy—is a mouthful, but understanding it fundamentally changed how we approached building practice programs for our students. In basic terms, nonlinear pedagogy is a branch of motor learning that establishes humans as complex and dynamic systems that are always changing and responding to their immediate environment with solutions to problems. There's obviously more to it than that—and entire books dedicated to explaining the scientific underpinnings of nonlinear pedagogy—but what matters is the concept's relevance to you and your game.

What does it mean for a golfer trying to get better?

It means you learn by doing the real thing: Creating a practice environment that gets as close as possible to the game— hitting real shots that matter—more often.

Why?

What stands out when you think of golf? Variability. It's a dynamic sport. You're always hitting different shots, in different conditions, with different kinds of emotions. If you aren't training yourself to handle this fundamental feature of the game, you're not training for the right sport.

Think of what golf "practice" entails for many people. It's

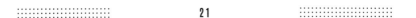

standing on a practice range with a perfect lie and an endless supply of balls.

That's not the game.

The disconnect is so great that any confidence you pick up in practice is irrelevant if you can't apply it to the game. The fact you can hit 10 perfect 7-irons in a row in practice doesn't matter if you can't hit one on the 16th green. It isn't because your skills are bad. It's because your training is failing you. You're developing solutions to two different tasks.

It is more helpful to your performance and confidence to be able to transition successfully from driver to 7-iron, back to driver and then onto another iron. Once solid contact and functional direction are established, the ability to adapt to different clubs, conditions, and shot requirements becomes the key skill you need to grow.

Creating a practice program that replicates the diverse challenges of the real game, and changes the challenges presented to the player based on how they perform, you do a very powerful thing. You'll create a more relevant base of confidence, as you'll be excelling in a task that is more like golf as it is played on the course.

You'll be out there practicing because you want to—because it's fun, and it's productive.

Golf is filled with plenty of tales of players beating thousands of balls—like Hogan finding it in the dirt—and plenty of people attach a kind of nobility to that struggle.

But let's face facts.

If your practice is a perpetual grind, and yields marginal results, slogging your way through it won't do much to make you want to commit the time and attention to work on your game.

Eventually, you're going to be more interested in watching a football game, hanging out with your kids or doing something else entertaining than you are beating balls relentlessly at the range, chasing a goal that doesn't seem to be getting any closer to you.

As teachers and coaches, our job is give you the tools that make you (in the words of two of *our* favorite teachers, Pia Nilsson and Lynn Marriott) your own best teacher. That happens when you're clear on what you're doing—which we're about to talk about—and you're enjoying the process.

FINDING YOUR CHALLENGE POINT

T HINK BACK TO ONE OF THE CLASSES you had in high school or college that was in a subject where you just didn't have much strength.

If you sat down in that class on the first day and the teacher dumped a mountain of intimidating and confusing information on you right away, you'd probably get discouraged pretty fast. That discouragement usually leads to giving up, and you never learn the material.

At the opposite end of the spectrum, if you went into the classroom with a kindergartener, it might be cute to sit and listen to the lessons for an hour, especially if your kid is in the class. But after a full day of hearing slow teacher-speak and basic lessons, you'd probably get fidgety and tune out. It's information you already know, and it isn't presenting a challenge.

It's easy to see the parallels in golf. Plenty of players get

overwhelmed by instruction—either because they're trying to sort it all out themselves, or they're not having the right interactions with an instructor during a lesson. The new information never gets integrated, and just falls away. You've probably seen it (or experienced yourself) in a lesson for a beginner, where all of the advice just piles on top of itself: Wider stance, different grip, swing it back this way, turn this way, don't lift your head. Sometimes it's amazing that the ball even gets hit.

The other side is just as important, and that's where a lot of dedicated players stall in their development. Maybe you've had some good instruction and you've played for a number of years, but you haven't been able to translate skills from the practice range to the course—or you have trouble with your game when you're under pressure. In those cases, you haven't been challenging yourself enough to promote the skill development it takes to make that jump.

Two researchers decided to figure out where the sweet spot of a skill development challenge really is—the *challenge* point that is the perfect combination of test and positive reinforcement. It's a practice task that is hard enough to keep you engaged and trying to master it, but not too hard so that it would be overwhelming.

The framework Drs. Mark Guadagnoli and Tim Lee created provides a way for teachers and coaches to optimize the level of difficulty of a task. It allows people to determine what too hard and too easy, are, and to adapt practice programs midstream. In English, it means you, the player, are challenged more effectively. You'll be able to scale a task such that it addresses your needs—both physically and psychologically—with the net result being you spending more time on the right

tasks, creating more confidence, and wasting less time.

We'll talk more in Chapter 4 about what this actually looks like on the practice tee, but don't worry—it's a fairly straightforward process. With any task, we are trying to do two things: Balance how "golf-like" the task is and how difficult it is for the learner to execute. We call this environmental stability and relative task difficulty. By combining these two elements in different amounts, we can dial in an optimal learning environment that is based on the immediate needs of the learner.

Using the range example again, a practice area at a really nice facility on a beautiful day is the essence of a stable environment. It has perfect lies, orderly targets, and unlimited balls to hit either to the same target or no target at all.

The least stable environment would be a player hitting various clubs from various lies to all kinds of different targets. The player might also be going through a pre-shot routine for each one and scoring himself or herself according to how well it was executed.

You know, like golf.

For task difficulty, it's the simple act of establishing the rules of the game to define what "success" is. It might be a single rule—hit your driver left of that pole. Or it could be many complicated ones—hit a 7-iron flighted below the roof of the clubhouse, and make it curve no more than 10 yards to the left. You choose the level of task difficulty required to achieve the skill development you're shooting for.

To conceptualize how you might go about combining the right amount of task difficulty with an appropriate amount of environmental stability, we use a framework that we call the Task Design Matrix. Depending on the needs of our client, it

helps us deliver tasks that are most likely to hit their learning sweetspot. The four quadrants of the Task Design Matrix are described below:

1. CLARIFY THE CONCEPT

THIS IS WHEN we need deliver a technical intervention. The instructions a player is delivering to the ball are not producing functional results. So we need to simplify the environment as much as possible to isolate whatever element of technique that needs improvement. This is typically where we start with a beginner with no concept of what to do with the club, or a player with an ingrained, but not very functional technique.

The goal is for you to gain a better understanding of what you're doing and how it compares to what you *should* be doing. So many golfers hit a good shot and have no idea what they need to do to reproduce it. When they hit a bad one, they don't know what went wrong. That's when paring down the difficulty and instability of tasks can be helpful.

What skill are you actually trying to learn? Are you clear on what you need to do, and do you know when you're doing it right or wrong?

Here's a common example. Say you have a massive slice that shows up on the tee, and you have no idea how to fix it. For this, the first step is to clarify concept.

What about the club delivery is producing the miss?

In this case, the face is pointing too far to the right of the path. This discrepancy between face and path is the concept the player needs to understand.

The way out is to experiment with different ways to produce an opposite result—a face that's closed to the path. This new swing might produce a pull hook at first, but the goal isn't to hit perfect shots. It's to concentrate on using one club from the same lie on the same shot and getting one sensation. The task is pretty easy, and the directive is simple and straightforward.

Once you gain that understanding of your big miss, you're on the way to self-diagnosing and self-coaching on the course. This is the first step—doing it on the range. Now it's time to add new levels of difficulty.

2. ADAPT AND CONQUER

ONE ESSENTIAL PIECE of skill development often gets overlooked. So many golfers practice one way of performing a shot, but when they get to the course, they aren't ready to make the subtle changes to their technique required for the demands of a certain situation. Our students hear it from us a lot: If all you have is a hammer, everything looks like a nail.

The best players don't have one solution to use for an on-course situation. They have many.

Once you've developed the base version of a skill to an acceptable level, it's time to take it and use it for a variety of situations. For example, you might use the same short game shot to attack a variety of different lies and hole locations, or use a variety of different shots to go at the same pin.

3. BUILD BELIEF

IF YOU ASKED EVERY GOLFER you know if confidence is an important element to their performance on the course, you would get a resounding and unanimous answer.

Of course it is.

If that's the case, why do so few golfers take action to develop this essential component? You work on your ball-striking skills, short game and putting. You should be spending equal time developing practice strategies designed specifically to improve your confidence on the course.

To do this with our students, we decrease the difficulty of a practice task while adding more instability to it.

For example, partial wedge shots can produce uncertainty because you're not comfortable with a specific distance. How much speed will you need to produce to hit a shot 63 yards instead of, say, 71? We lay out a set of cones in ten yard increments from 30 to 100 yards, and prescribe tasks designed to answer those questions.

Our players walk up to those scoring shots on the course with the swagger and certainty that only come from practice aimed specifically at building belief.

Even if that's all you did—practicing to build that "I got this" attitude—you'd be better off than if you spent all your time grinding away on some specific mechanical element of your technique.

4. TAKE IT TO THE COURSE

THIS IS WHERE SKILLS get integrated into your on-course game. In traditional practice, you're doing the same things to solve the same problems over and over again. This can help you refine your technique, but it doesn't do much to get you ready for the course—where you get one chance to make the right decision and hit the best shot.

Instead of practicing the same solution over and over, we want you to practice *finding* the solutions. This means spreading balls out over different random lies and going through the process of picking shots and executing them just as you would on the course. The shots are hard and the environment is unstable, because we're working hard to transfer those skills into your real game.

Chapter 4 is filled with great challenges that will specifically help you do this. As you succeed through the different levels of these games, you'll be systematically building what we call a "performer psychology"—a mindset that has intense focus on processes and solutions, not just individual mechanics.

• • •

What happens at the end of this journey—when you've found a practice plan that clicks? You enter what the researchers in psychology call a state of flow. It's when you become so engrossed in what you're doing that you don't notice time clicking by. According to an extremely influential study by Dr. Mihaly Csikszentmihalyi for his book, *Flow: The Psychology of Optimal Experience*, athletes and other performers get into the flow

state (or the zone, as you've probably heard of it on sports TV) when they are able to focus on one thing and give their total attention to it. The task at hand is challenging enough to demand their full attention—not boring or so challenging that success would be almost unlikely.

To see this all happen in front of you, on a little stage, watch a teenager play a video game he or she is totally engrossed in. The game makers are geniuses at producing the perfect challenge points and feedback loops for players—cycles that offer hard-but-not-impossible obstacles, instant feedback about how you're doing and progressive levels of difficulty. The games are *designed* to get a player hooked by the exact brain mechanisms designed to absorb new information. (For a fascinating look at how those games are made, and how they are changing the way we think, check out *Reality is Broken*, by Jane McGonigal.)

There really is a kind of switch in our heads that engages us in "peak learning." But it does come with an important condition that is almost impossible to trick or fake out.

The task also has to *matter*. Apathy is worse than boredom. If you don't care about what you're doing, and it doesn't matter to you if you get better or not, you're not going have the motivation and attitude it takes to get into that flow.

Need proof? Watch that same video game teenager who has no interest in golf get sent to a lesson against his or her will. We've seen it hundreds of times at our facilities. That's a mountain even the best teacher in history would have a hard time climbing.

We're going to assume you're here because you want to be (you bought the book, after all!). And all of the research and

observation of people doing lots of other things besides golf is nice, but what does it look like when it's put in practice, for actual golfers?

Does it actually work?

You're not getting some beta testing version of *Better Faster*. The practice plans and strategies in this book have been fully developed from the programs we've put in place in Texas and California. They've produced Division I college players, tour golfers, club champions—and just plain old happy-to-be-five-shots-better players.

The proof is in the results. And now it's your turn.

CHAPTER 3

THE ASSESSMENT:
WHAT DO YOU DO TODAY,
AND WHAT DO YOU NEED?

WHY ARE YOUR SCORES WHAT THEY ARE? Everybody has some baseline assumptions they make about their own skills. If somebody asked you, you might say you don't get off the tee very well, but your short game is good and you're a terrific putter. Or you might say that you hit your driver and fairway woods great, but you struggle when you play from the rough. Or you're a good all-around player but you're really bad on the greens.

Again, those descriptions can be pretty true, but just like your *real* handicap index, they need some rational, realistic assessment.

Are you really as bad as you think off the tee? Is your putting as good as you think it is, especially when you have to hole everything out?

Is there another part of your game that you don't give as much thought to—bunker play, strategy, trouble shots—where you really cost yourself strokes?

We've found that most players tend to report their own strengths and weaknesses in a way that is colored with bias and emotion. They have a hard time forming an objective opinion about what they really do on the course. It can happen for a variety of reasons. More recent results can skew their perception. They can overreact to weaknesses and think of them as worse than they really are. They can downplay strengths and not see the true value of some skills.

They have blind spots. Most of us do.

Our objective is to help you streamline your practice process and get more out of the time you spend at it. The first step in that process is to figure out where you're starting from. That means taking stock of where you really are with your skills. Why? The only way to apply practice most efficiently is to apply it to the skills that need the most work.

In other words, you can't move toward mastery if you don't know where you stand on the scale. You need a baseline.

When we first meet with a new client, our first task is to complete an assessment and take stock of their current skills. This information we gather during this initial meeting serves as a baseline that informs the direction we go. It gives us a game plan for where to start and a path to close the gaps between the game they have and the game they want—and, a lot of times, it gives the student some new information about his or her game.

In this chapter, we're going to set you up to take your own self-guided assessment. At the end of it, you'll have a very accurate inventory of your game. From there, you'll be able to take the results and select the perfect practice plan (or plans) for your game.

For example, you might see that the most glaring weakness in your game is your ballstriking. You'll be able to use the practice plan specifically for ballstriking, and improve both your skills and the application of those skills. We will also help you dig deeper into each area. While you may already know that ballstriking is your issue, there are several different aspects to the skill—different pieces to the puzzle. Our goal is to help you isolate the ones that should be your biggest priority, and attack them with energy and focus.

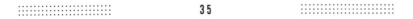

The best part about the assessment questionnaire—and the practice plans themselves—is that they're completely adaptable to your skill level and needs. Using the previous example, you might find that what you think might be a strong suit may be a weakness, or vice-versa. Our goal is to ensure that one thing is clear; that you learn from the assessment where *all* of your skills stand, and where you need to invest time and energy in order to improve.

You can then work your way through any (and all) of the plans, improving each area of your game. You might be a B+ driver of the ball and a C- iron player, but you'll now be able to pinpoint which elements you need to develop to raise your grade. You'll make more informed decisions when organizing your practice, and work on the right things more often.

We've structured this self-guided assessment to be similar to the ones we conduct with our clients in person. It follows the framework of the Task Design Matrix we described in Chapter 2. It lays out the path to mastery, and identifies your current position on that path.

There are three different assessments—one for full swing, one for putting and one for your wedge game. You can take the tests in any order, either sequentially or based on which part of your game you think needs to most help. Regardless of where you choose to start, we encourage you to complete all three. That way, you'll get the best look at your overall game. The results just might surprise you.

Once you get the results, your scores will point you toward specific categories of practice we discussed in Chapter 2— clarifying concept, diversifying skill set, building belief and transferring skill. In the next chapter, we lay out the specific practice plans for part of the game. Within those plans, you'll see exactly where you need to plug in the assessment results.

FULL SWING: 21-BALL TEST

WHAT IS THE FUNDAMENTAL SKILL you're trying to master in this game? Hitting the ball where you want it to go. This assessment will track how well you control the three main aspects of a shot—the quality of the strike, the start direction of the ball and the ball's curvature.

Quality of strike is slightly subjective. We want to know the answer to the following question: Did you catch the shot flush and clean, or was it slightly thin or fat, heeled or toed? Be sure to judge yourself critically. Grading the quality of your strike better than it really is just holds you back from improving.

Start line is the direction, relative to target, that the ball leaves the face. For a straight shot, that line would be straight toward the target. On a fade, it would leave on a vector slightly left of the target line. A draw would leave slightly to the right. We want to see how closely reality matches intent.

Curve direction is relatively straightforward. Your goal is to determine if you are able to make the ball curve. Can you move it right to left on command? How about left to right? Notice that the assessment says "draw" and "fade"—not "hook" and "slice." The goal is to have you develop control over both the type of curve you put on the ball, as well as the amount of that curve!

Go through the progression of shots listed below with your

7-iron and driver, and record the result for each shot. Each time you make quality contact, start the ball on the right line and make it curve the right way, you get a point for each one of those achievements. For example, it you make quality contact, but start the ball left of your intended line and it has the wrong curvature, you'd only collect the one point from making good contact.

The last set of balls for each club is what we call the "gamer" section. You hit three balls with your "go-to" swing, and measure how well you execute on your intent. We hope that your scores are highest on this set. If not, that tells you that you don't really have a stock shot!

TEST BASICS

I. USING A 7-IRON, hit four sets of three balls according to the rules on the next page. The goal is to hit three identical shots for each set.

2. FOR EACH SHOT, record one point for successfully making solid contact, starting the ball on the right line, and making the ball curve the right direction.

3. USING A DRIVER, hit three sets of three balls according to the rules below.

4. THE LAST THREE BALLS for each club should represent stock shots with each club.

5. AS YOU PROGRESS, you can substitute different irons and woods for the 7 and driver.

CLUB	SHOT	STRIKE	START	CURVE
7-IRON	DRAW			
	DRAW			
	DRAW			
	FADE			
	FADE			
	FADE			
	LOW			
	MEDIUM			
	HIGH			
	GAMER			
	GAMER			
	GAMER			

CLUB	SHOT	STRIKE	START	CURVE
DRIVER	DRAW			
	DRAW			
	DRAW			
	FADE			
	FADE			
	FADE			
	GAMER			
	GAMER			
	GAMER			

ANALYZING YOUR SCORE:

BY TOTALING YOUR SCORE for each column—contact, start line and curve—you will quickly find your most troublesome area. With your weakest area in mind, follow the mental map below to figure out where you stand in your skill development—and where you should start in the practice plan.

If there is very little difference from one column to the next, you can follow the general list of priorities we use with our students:

I. START WITH A SOLID STRIKE.

Until you're hitting shots solidly, you don't want to start layering on other requirements, like start line and curve. Are you missing the center of the face, or is your swing bottoming out in the wrong place?

2. MOVE TO PREDICTABLE CURVE.

Once you can hit the ball solidly in of the middle of the face with ball-first, ground second contact, you can work on making subtle adjustments to your stock shot to change the ball's curve.

3. FINISH WITH CONTROLLING AND GENERATING DISTANCE.

The final piece of the puzzle is not just maximizing your distance with each club, but rather, hitting clubs specific distances. We want to have command over power and precision. We're looking for more yardage with acceptable accuracy in the driver, and tighter dispersions with the scoring clubs.

WHAT'S THE BALLSTRIKING PRACTICE PLAN FOR YOU?

START HERE

ARE YOU ABOUT TO PLAY AN IMPORTANT ROUND?

NO

YES

NO

FOR THE MOST PART, DO YOU UNDERSTAND WHY YOUR MISSES OCCUR?

ARE YOU IN CODE RED PANIC MODE?

YES

NO

CLARIFY CONCEPT

BUILD BELIEF

YES

ARE YOU ABLE TO SELF-COACH THE SOLUTION?

NO

DIVERSIFY SKILL SET

YES

NO

CAN YOU MAKE SLIGHT ADJUSTMENTS TO YOU 'STOCK' SWING TO CHANGE TRAJECTORY, DISTANCE AND CURVE?

NO

TRANSFER SKILL

YES

CAN YOU TAKE YOUR 'RANGE' GAME TO THE COURSE?

YES

BLENDED PLAN
10% CC
30% DS
30% BB
30% TS

PUTTING: 9-HOLE PUTTING COURSE

PUTTING MIGHT BE THE MOST satisfying game element to work on, because the feedback is so immediate. Fundamentally, the ball goes in the hole because you picked the right target, hit the ball at that target and did it with the right speed. The goal here is to get a clear picture of how well you do those three things—and where you should be investing your practice time.

The way we do this is with a straightforward nine-hole putting course. You'll be measuring the quality of your approach putts both in terms of speed and read in addition to how well you hole out shorter putts when there are consequences for a miss.

TEST BASICS

I. CREATE A PUTTING COURSE featuring nine different putts ranging in distance from three to 30 feet. Pace off the distances accurately, and vary the order in which you hit the putts so that you aren't hitting putts of similar distance, break or elevation change, consecutively.

2. FOR EACH PUTT, place a dime one your selected line two feet ahead of the ball.

3. HIT EACH PUTT. If you roll the ball over the dime, check the appropriate box on the scorecard.

4. IF YOUR PUTT MISSES, but ends less than two feet from the hole, check the box for "Good speed."

5. IF YOU HIT THE DIME but the putt finishes either short and within a grip length on the low side of the cup, or past the hole and outside of two feet, but in line with the hole, give yourself a check in the 'Good read' column.

6. PUTT OUT EACH HOLE and record your score.

7. SUBTRACT YOUR SCORE from the Shots to Hole column and record that number in the Strokes Gained column. For exam-

ple, if you one-putted the 3-foot putt, you would gain 0.053 strokes. A two-putt would cost you 0.947 strokes.

HOLE	DISTANCE	SHOTS TO HOLE	SCORE	SGP (SHOTS TO HOLE- SCORE)	HIT COIN?	GOOD SPEED?	READ?
1	3	1.053					
2	21	1.891					
3	12	1.705					
4	6	1.357					
5	27	1.953					
6	9	1.575					
7	15	1.79					
8	18	1.848					
9	30	1.978					

SGP	0

ANALYZING YOUR SCORE:

H OW MANY PUTTS did it take you to complete the course? Beyond your overall score, what was your total strokes gained score? Strokes gained is valuable, because it penalizes you for putts you should be making, while being tolerant of lower-percentage misses.

You can also look deeper than the cumulative stats and see how well you're hitting your preferred line and controlling your speed. You can also see connections between the individual skills and their combined effect—the resulting score. How often are you two- and three-putting when you miss your line, or fail to control your speed?

Add up your results in each column—start line, speed and read. Once you've tabulated your results , work your way through the mental map below to find out where you need to start. As with full swing, try to identify the aspect of your putting that has the potential to yield the greatest gain. Where did you score the lowest? This will be your jumping off point when creating your practice plan.

If you don't have a clear area of weakness, follow this general priority list.

1. START WITH START LINE.

Gaining control over the face of the putter is the most important skill to master. If you can't control the face, you can't control direction, which will make it very hard to hole putts.

2. CONTROL YOUR SPEED.

Once you have a handle on the face, you can start to modulate the length and speed of your stroke to change distance.

3. LEARN TO READ GREENS.

Understanding and adapting to green contours is a learnable skill. It takes a plan, practice, and feedback.

FINESSE WEDGES: 9-SHOT TEST

L IKE PUTTING, GREENSIDE WEDGE PLAY is a segement of the game that offers an opportunity for most golfers to save strokes. When we look at what's required to have a great short game, or what great wedge players are able to do, it is control the distance, trajectory, and spin of the ball. Unifying these skills lets elite short game players get the ball closer to the hole from a variety of situations.

To establish a starting point for your training and to test the strength of your arsenal around the greens, you'll be asked to successfully match distance and trajectory from a variety of situations. By varying distance and trajectory, and by seeing how closely the outcome of the shot match-

es your intention, we can get a clearer picture of where your strengths and weaknesses lie.

TEST BASICS

1. SET UP A SERIES OF NINE PITCH SHOTS—three each from 10, 15 and 20 yards from the target.

2. PLAY A HIGH, MEDIUM AND LOW SHOT to the target from each set of three balls, making sure to vary the kind of lie and target you use. You might not have room to use a different hole for each target, but do your best to vary the kinds of shots you hit.

3. FOR EACH SHOT, PICK A LANDING SPOT and mark it with a tee in the ground. If you come within one yard of the landing spot on your shot, mark the appropriate box on the scorecard.

4. AFTER EACH SHOT, evaluate it for the quality of contact and accuracy of predicted trajectory. Remember, it's better to be a harder grader than an easier one.

5. FINALLY, RECORD THE DISTANCE LEFT to the hole after your shot. This is an important metric, because PGA Tour players make 70 percent of their putts from six feet, while they make only 50 percent from eight feet.

6. CALCULATE YOUR AVERAGE PUTT LENGTH by adding all of the putt lengths left after each shot and dividing by nine. Also, tabulate your results for the number of times you hit your landing spot, made good contact, and achieved your intended trajectory.

TRAJECTORY	DISTANCE	PROXIMITY	HIT SPOT?	HIT TRAJECTORY?	GOOD CONTACT?
LOW	10				
	15				
	20				
	TOTAL				
MEDIUM	10				
	15				
	20				
	TOTAL				
HIGH	10				
	15				
	20				
	TOTAL				

ANALYZING YOUR RESULTS:

ASK YOURSELF the following question: Where is the inconsistency coming from? Is it an inability to make consistent contact? Am I having a hard time hitting my landing spot? Am I hitting my landing spot and still not getting it close? Or are my shots coming out differently than I had planned? The answers will help guide you where you need to do your first work.

Once you've identified the weakest area for you—distance control, trajectory control, strike quality or landing precision—use the mental map below to assess that skill and where you should begin when planning your practice.

If there's no clear weakness, you can use this general guide to prioritize your work:

I. CONTACT IS KING.

Making clean contact is the first step in improving your performance.

2. DIAL IN YOUR TOUCH.

Once you've become proficient in hitting the ball solidly, you can expand your skills by learning to hit shots different distances.

3. LEARN TO FLIGHT IT.

The best wedge players are able to vary the trajectory of their short shots to successfully navigate any situation they may find themselves in.

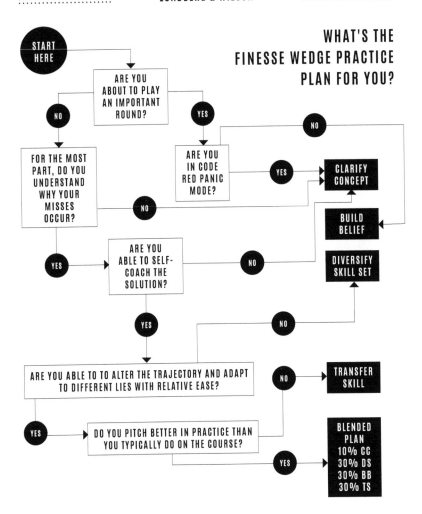

WHAT'S THE FINESSE WEDGE PRACTICE PLAN FOR YOU?

A POINT OF CAUTION: Don't get frustrated if your score starts out very low. Very few players have ever really taken stock of their game, or tried to hit shots "on purpose." Understanding this and committing to practicing the right things, the right way, is a big first step in your pursuit of improvement.

ONE LAST POINT: These assessments aren't designed to be

one-and-done. You should continue to use them regularly to keep track of your progress as well as the overall health of your skills. Over time, things change—even tour players go through stretches where they struggle with particular parts of their games. The assessments will help you quickly identify the avenues you need to take in order to get back on track.

That's how you get better, faster.

CHAPTER 4

THE SOLUTIONS:
PRACTICE TECHNIQUES AND PLANS
FOR EVERY PLAYER AND GOAL

NOW YOU KNOW where you stand. You can truly focus your practice and fast-track your improvement by getting right to the kind of personal practice you need to do for your level and your game. This comes in the form of tasks—specific exercises and drills you can follow to introduce, build and establish a variety of skills.

Remember, the mental maps from the previous chapter established where exactly you should dive in in each particular area—ball-striking, distance wedge play and putting:

→ CLARIFYING CONCEPT: For exploring a new skill in a safe, stable environment. The goal is to leave the tasks with a better understanding of the technical requirements to perform each skill.

→ DIVERSIFYING SKILL SET: For expanding your basic proficiency and adapting it to a variety of situations. Here, you'll have to create multiple solutions to the same problem in a stable environment. The goal is to leave these tasks with a thorough understanding of what it takes to produce those variations and the skills to execute them.

→ BUILDING BELIEF: For establishing your confidence in the baseline skills you've been establishing. Confidence comes from evidence. When you can see yourself execute a task with a successful outcome, you begin to believe you can do it when it matters. The atmosphere for these tasks is more dynamic—like the course, but not quite as difficult. The goal is to leave these tasks with the confidence you can perform with a high degree of relative success.

→ TRANSFERRING SKILL: For challenging your skills at the highest level, and replicating real golf as closely as possible. These are exercises that require the player to successfully adapt their base motion to constant changes in the environment. The goal here is to leave these tasks with far more comfort and flexibility when challenged with new and difficult situations.

To use these practice plans, find the shot category you're going to be working on—ball-striking, scrambling or putting, and find the skill entry point from your mental map assessment in the previous chapter.

Once you know where to start, follow the tasks from start to finish. As for how long you should perform each task before moving on, prescribing a size or duration of the dose isn't always so easy. We'd love to be able to say "Complete Drill X" this many times and you're cured." But golf doesn't work that way.

We like to view these practice plans as daily vitamins—to be taken consistently to correct and prevent major skill issues from materializing.

As we've been talking about, finding the right type of tasks isn't always a black and white process, and your progress will hardly ever happen in a clean, straight line. Time and effort does not always produce proportional progress. While that may be a frustrating reality—that we never truly master a skill in golf—it's also one of the greatest appeals of the game. Performance and confidence is always in a constant state of flux. We are always chasing 'better." That's true even for the best players in the game.

This means that you need to assess yourself frequently to figure out where to spend your time, and how to design your learning environment to optimize your tasks. Your mind maps in the previous chapter will be your greatest resource in navigating where to go and when. Refer to them often when planning out your practice session to make sure you make the most of your time. If you do, be assured that it's time well spent. Quality over quantity!

BALL-STRIKING

Clarifying Concept

I. SOLID STRIKE ZONE

→ *Overview:* The first goal in golf is to hit the ball solidly and send it where you aim. This task will help you learn how to deliver the club in a way that avoids the major contact errors—fat shots, thin shots, toe strikes and heel strikes.

→ *Environment:* Driving range, 8-iron

→ *Tools:* Tees, golf towel

→ *Design:* Place the towel flat on the ground six inches behind the ball, stick two tees in the ground on either side of the clubhead at address, and one tee in the ground two inches in front of the ball (toward the target), so that the tee head is barely showing out of the ground.

→ *Objective:* Swing the clubhead through the gates, miss the towel, achieve ball-first contact, and clip the forward tee. The tees provide feedback on where they club is bottom out, where on the face the ball is being struck, and the direction the club is travelling through impact.

→ *Completion Cue:* If you can successfully strike the ball and front tee while avoiding the gates and towel five times in a row, you've developed a clear concept for what's needed to strike solid iron shots. To be sure, complete a 10 ball set, striving for 80% success rate.

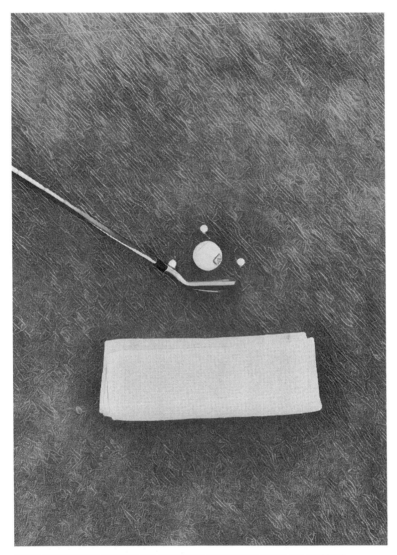

SWING THE CLUBHEAD THROUGH THE GATE WHILE MISSING THE TOWEL AND CLIPPING
THE FORWARD TEE. IF YOU START CREATING DEEP DIVOTS, YOU'VE LIKELY OVERDONE IT.

→ *Troubleshooting:* The most common problems with this task come from a faulty pivot or poor release timing. If you struggle to miss the towel and gate tees, practice first by making smaller, slower swings, and attempt to position more weight on your lead foot at impact. Once you complete the task successfully with smaller, slower swings, incrementally increase your speed until you get up to regular speed. Follow the 80% rule as you progress to bigger and faster swings. Start with a 10-ball set of slower half swings. If you strike eight of 10 solid, you know it's time to add speed or length of swing. The goal is to work your way up to a full speed, full length swing while achieving success 80% of the time.

2. DRAW STATION

→ *Overview:* Once you can make a consistent strike, the next step is increasing your command of the ball's curve. The relationship between where the face is pointing and where the club is swinging provides the ball instructions on how to curve. Shots that have a lot of curve are produced when there is a big difference between the angle of the face at impact and the path of the swing. Here you will develop your awareness of the clubface and swing path and how they make the ball curve.

→ *Environment:* Range, middle iron

→ *Tools:* Three alignment rods

→ *Design:* Place one rod on the target line two feet ahead of the ball, one rod two feet behind the ball angled 20 degrees from the target line toward you (pointing right of the target for right hand players) and the third rod one foot outside the ball parallel to the target line.

→ *Objective:* Develop a predictable curve by using the angled rod

ALIGN YOUR BODY PARALLEL TO THE TARGET LINE. IN YOUR DOWNSWING,
TRY TO GET THE SHAFT OF YOUR CLUB TO MATCH THE ANGLED STICK ON THE GROUND.
THIS WILL GET YOU INTO A POSITION FROM WHICH YOU CAN HIT A DRAW.

as a guide for your approach to the ball. The rod in front of the
ball serves as a guide to see where your ball starts, while the
rod to the outside of the target line offers a guide for alignment (of the clubface and body at address) while also providing additional reference for the target line.

For most players, we set this drill up to encourage a draw,
since a slice is the shot that plagues so many of our recreational
clients. If you're struggling with hooks, just shift the direction

of the angled shaft to the left of the target (for right handers).

→ *Completion Cue:* If you can hit eight out of 10 balls that start to the right of the target line and curve left, you have graduated from this drill.

→ *Troubleshooting:* If ball is curving too much, or isn't curving the way you predict, you still have a discrepancy between where the face and the path are aimed at impact. To fix it, break the task into two parts. First, concentrate on creating left curve by having the face pointed left of your path. This may produce some large pull hooks, but by doing this on purpose you're on the right track. Once you can reliably produce a left curve, start attempting to move the start line of the ball to the right by changing your swing direction more to the right and getting the face pointing slightly right of target at impact. Spend time calibrating these two parts, and then go back to the original task. We've also found it helpful to alternate between hitting a shot that starts left and curves left, with one that starts more right and falls left.

3. SPEED EXPLORATIONS

→ *Overview:* Your relationship to distance has two pieces—increasing the available distance you can hit the ball, and controlling the distance you can hit each club so that shots become more predictable. Distance comes from a variety of factors, but clubhead speed is the easiest one for you to control and change. This task will help you understand the different ways to control your speed.

→ *Environment:* Range, middle iron

→ *Tools:* None

→ *Design:* None

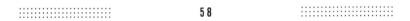

→ *Objective:* Use different combinations of three variables to explore their combined effects on distance: A) backswing length, B) effective shaft length—how far you choke up or down on the handle, and C) tempo. Hit ten shots with your normal grip, backswing length and tempo. Hit 10 more balls where you alter one of these principles. Take note of what the change does to your distance. Go through the exercise three times, each time changing a different element.

→ *Completion Cue:* You can move on when you're able to hit five consecutive shots with the same club that travel shorter than the previous shot by combining or manipulating the three speed control elements.

→ *Troubleshooting:* Most players are able to catch on to this task pretty quickly. However, if it becomes a struggle, the likely culprits are either dynamic loft, or quality of contact. Dynamic loft is the amount of loft you deliver at impact. It influences how much of the club's energy gets into the ball, how high the ball launches, and how much the ball spins. These factors, along with making precise contact in the middle of the face, are key contributors to distance. If shots are coming up high and short, you're likely presenting too much dynamic loft, and/or not making great contact. This makes it difficult to consistently gauge and control distance. If your results are erratic, we would recommend that you go back to Solid Strike Zone, as it promotes more functional delivery of loft. Once you're succeeding at an 80% success rate, come back to this task and begin to explore the other elements we described to change clubhead speed.

Diversifying Skill Set

I. VARIABLE SOLID STRIKE ZONE

→ *Overview:* In the first stage of this task, you learned how to brush the grass in front of the ball. Now, your job is to expand on this task through the bag. Repeating a basic task with consistent specifications is an important first step, but now we're going to start moving the bar. In this exercise, you'll use random clubs and try to replicate the solid contact you produced in the initial segment of this task.

→ *Environment:* Range, all clubs from 3-wood to wedge

→ *Tools:* Tees, golf towel

→ *Design:* Just as you did in Solid Strike Zone, place a towel flat on the ground six inches behind the ball and stick two tees in the ground on either side of the clubhead. Put a third tee in the ground two inches in front of the ball, with the head barely sticking up above the ground.

→ *Objective:* The goal is the same as the first edition of this task: Strike the ball first and the front tee second, while missing the towel and the guide tees. This time, pick a random club for each of the ten shots within the set.

→ *Completion Cue:* If you can successfully strike the ball and front tee while avoiding the gate and the towel on eight of 10 shots for the set, you've expanded your striking capabilities throughout the bag.

→ *Troubleshooting:* If you're having trouble getting to eight with certain clubs, try reducing the frequency with which you change clubs. First, try using two clubs to complete the task. Then progress to three, four, etc. If you're still struggling, return to the solid strike task in the first segment.

2. TRIDENT

→ *Overview:* When you can make the ball curve in both directions, you increase your ability to self-coach and self-correct on the fly. When the ball is curving too much in one direction, you know how to adapt to reduce that curve. This task will help you modulate the dramatic curves you hit in the first edition of this task. By producing softer curves, you'll be able to hit your shots more on target.

→ *Environment:* Range, all clubs

→ *Tools:* Three alignment rods

→ *Design:* Place an alignment rod in front of your ball, down the target line, another in line and inside the first rod but angled 20 degrees to the left of the target and the third in line and outside of the first rod but angled 20 degrees right of the target. You will have created a "trident" of rods point at the target, left of it and right of it.

→ *Objective:* The goal here is to expand your ability to create predictable curves by forcing you to produce them on command. Start by hitting a cut shot to your target. For a right handed golfer, this means you'll want to shift the direction your club travels through impact to match the leftward pointing rod while pointing the face somewhere between the left rod and the target line rod at impact. Next, try to draw it at your target by doing the opposite. Shift your club direction to match up with the rightward pointing rod while pointing the face between the right rod and the target line rod at impact.

→ *Completion Cue:* If you can create the intended curvature and get the ball to finish within reasonable proximity of your target in eight out of 10 attempts, you've graduated from this task.

→ *Troubleshooting:* If you struggle to complete this task, it's prob-

TRIDENT

ALIGNMENT RODS
ON GROUND IN
FRONT OF BALL

START THE BALL BETWEEN THE OUTSIDE STICK AND THE MIDDLE
STICK, AND TRY TO CURVE IT TO THE MIDDLE STICK.

ably because you have excessive club path or face orientation
that makes it hard to hit one of the two shot types. Go back to
the first edition of this task and develop more command of the
opposite shot shape from the one you're comfortable playing.

3. HOPSCOTCH

→ *Overview:* You will rarely get "perfect" yardages when you're
playing. Most shots will be some percentage less than full. So
it is crucial to develop distance control with every club. By ex-

panding your capacity to control distance beyond your wedges, you will be able to maximize your scoring potential. This task will bring you more precision with your longer clubs, as well as the traditional scoring clubs.

→ *Environment:* Range, all clubs

→ *Tools:* None

→ *Design:* Use three balls. Hit one that what you would call full speed, and note where it lands. On the next ball, hit what you consider a 75-percent shot and note where it lands. On the third ball, try to land your shot between the first two shots. Take note of how much speed you think that shot required. If you don't land the third shot in between the first two, try again to land one in between until you succeed.

→ *Objective:* Complete this three-distance exercise which one short club (pitching wedge through 8-iron), one middle iron (7, 6 or 5-iron), and one hybrid/fairway wood.

→ *Completion Cue:* If you can complete the challenge with each club and do it within five balls, you are increasing your under-

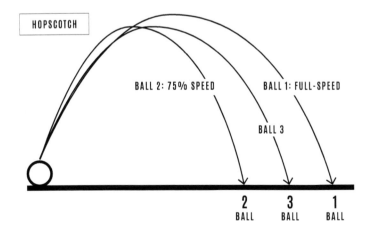

standing of how force is regulated, and you've expanded your swing motion to produce more command of distance.

→ *Troubleshooting:* Distance control problems usually come from poor contact, difficulties in controlling dynamic loft at impact, or a lack of awareness of speed. If your contact is solid, go back to the first level of this exercise and spend more time building your command over the speed element you feel most confident in manipulating when tasked with changing how far you need to hit your clubs. If solid contact is the issue, spend more time on Solid Strike Zone to develop more control of the bottom of your swing.

Building Belief

I. AROUND THE HORN

→ *Overview:* Once you've learned to make a great strike through the bag from a basic, good lie, it's time to challenge yourself with different lies and stances. Learning the subtle adaptions that make those shots easier to play is a big step. Ranges are mostly flat, so how do you practice those subtle adaptations? By creating an environment for it, complete with feedback.

→ *Environment:* Range, 7-iron

→ *Tools:* Six tees

→ *Design:* Place your ball on a low tee and stick five tees low in the ground in half-circle around the ball—outside the toe, the heel and a clubhead width behind the ball.

→ *Objective:* Address the first inside tee, but swing with the intent of hitting the ball on the middle tee with a centered strike. Work your way around the five outside tees, addressing them and then hitting the ball from the center tee. This requires precise clubface awareness, and the ability to make swing adjust-

ADDRESS THE FIRST INSIDE TEE, BUT SWING WITH THE INTENT OF
HITTING THE BALL ON THE MIDDLE TEE WITH A CENTERED STRIKE.
TRY THE SAME THING USING THE OTHER TEES AS A STARTING POINT.

ments to hit the ball solid despite less than ideal setup conditions. This is a great way to warm up your proprioception
(special awareness), and reduce fat, thin, toe and heel hits.
Reference this warm-up drill when you notice on the course
that you're tending to mishit shots and you'll be able to quickly find a solution.

→ *Completion Cue:* If you can successfully strike the middle ball solidly from all five address positions, you can check the box on your ability to hit solid iron shots, and you can approach your round with confidence and self-belief.

→ *Troubleshooting:* Players will tend to struggle with certain tee starting points—either the inside tees or outside tees. Take note of the locations that give you the most trouble and devote some extra repetitions to them. Grow your awareness for what you need to feel to create solid strikes from these trouble positions. This will develop your spatial awareness, and improve the quality of your strikes.

2. TWO-SHAPE CHALLENGE

→ *Overview:* When you know that you're able to control the curve of your shots, you're going to play with tremendous confidence. That knowledge (and confidence) comes from practicing in a way that offers feedback about your skills being on (or off) point. This task will challenge you to produce difference shot shapes while maintaining a level of performance.

→ *Environment:* Range

→ *Tools:* Clubs

→ *Design:* Select three targets. One should be reachable by a short iron, the next a middle iron and third a hybrid.

→ *Objective:* Pick one of the targets. Hit one shot that flies right to left and one shot that flies left to right, with both landing within certain proximity of the target. You can complete this task with your driver as well, as long as you pick a landing zone approximately 35 yards wide.

→ *Completion Cue:* If you're able to achieve the desired outcome in three or fewer shots with each club, you will have confirmation that you can play those shots without fear on the course.

→ *Troubleshooting:* Take note of the shot shapes that give you the most trouble, and go back to the trident drill to develop your awareness of the path and face relationships that will produce that shot. If you're struggling with your trajectory, explore different ball positions to help you apply the appropriate amount of loft to produce the desired launch angle and height.

3. GREEN SCALES

→ *Overview:* When you practice, you usually gravitate toward clubs you like to hit, and ones you have the most confidence in. Want evidence? Look at the faces of your irons and see which ones are the most worn out. This task will expand your comfort and confidence to other clubs and distances.

→ *Environment:* Range

→ *Tools:* Clubs

→ *Design:* Select five targets on the range. Each target should vary in length so that you'll never hit the same club twice.

→ *Objective:* The goal is to land a shot within 10 percent shot distance of the target—meaning, if you're hitting 125 yard shot, you need to land the ball within 12.5 yards of the target. Once you've landed the ball within the required distance of the first target, then you can move on to the second target. If you move to the second target and then fail to get a ball within the 10 percent target distance, you have to move to the previous target and complete that task again.

→ *Completion Cue:* If you're able to hit the required shots within the required distance from each target within 7 balls, you should be confident in your ability to play any approach shot with a high degree of precision.

→ *Troubleshooting:* If you're experiencing difficulty with a specific shot, determine if it is a distance/contact issue, or a direction/face and path issue, and revisit the appropriate task in the previous sections.

Transferring Skill

I. TEE SHOT MATRIX

→ *Overview:* Functional tee shot accuracy—the combination of distance and accuracy—is closely correlated to the expected score you will make on a hole. How? It influences the difficulty of your next shot. Think about it, which shot is easier? An 8 iron from the fairway, or a 4 iron out of the rough? The longer and straighter you can hit your tee shots, or the more command you can have over your driver, the easier the game will be. This task will help you develop more control over your tee shots, regardless of the club you use, and help you perform under some pressure.

→ *Environment:* Range or course

→ *Tools:* Driver

CLUB	MISS BIG FWY LEFT	MISS BIG FWY LEFT OF CENTER	HIT SMALL CENTER OF FAIRWAY	HIT BIG FWY RIGHT OF CENTER	MISS BIG FAIRWAY RIGHT
DRIVER (+1/2)	-1/2 POINT	+1/2 POINT	+1 POINT	+1/2 POINT	-1/2 POINT
SECONDARY (0)	-1 POINT	0 POINTS	+1/2 POINT	0 POINTS	-1 POINT
3RD STRING (-1/2)	-1.5 POINTS	-1/2 POINT	0 POINTS	-1/2 POINT	-1.5 POINTS

→ *Design:* Designate a 35-yard wide fairway on the range. Inside the fairway, identify a smaller fairway, approximately 20 yards wide. Ration out 14 golf balls. Hit eight with the driver, four with the secondary club, two with your third choice. Score each ball using the scoring matrix on page 68. Keep track of your points.

You may adjust the fairway sizes to align with your skill level. The better the golfer you are, the smaller the fairways, and conversely, the less-skilled a golfer you are, the bigger your fairways can be. If you're completing the task on the golf course, chart the finishing position of your tee shots and tally your points per the scoring matrix.

→ *Objective:* Unite decision-making and physical skills to facilitate optimal performance in true golf conditions.

Completion Cue: If you are scoring more than four points, you are demonstrating a high level of length and accuracy off the tee.

→ *Troubleshooting:* If you're having difficulty scoring points, quarantine the variable that you believe to be the cause, and train it in isolation under more stable conditions.

2. FIVE PERCENT CHALLENGE

→ *Overview:* To be a great iron player, you need to control the distance and direction of the ball. The Five Percent Challenge challenges your ability to manage the outcome of the shot while layering on shape requirements and a randomized order.

→ *Environment:* Driving range with targets, or golf course

→ *Tools:* Balls

→ *Design:* Hit 18 shots of varying distances. On each shot, change either the trajectory or curve, or both. Never hit the same shot twice.

→ *Objective:* Your goal is to execute the shot as required AND have the ball finish within five percent of the shot distance from the cup (for example, on a 180-yard shot, the five percent radius would be nine yards). As you go through the exercise, keep track of how many shots finish inside that five percent radius.

→ *Completion Cue:* If you're able to have more than 60% of your shots finish inside the radius from the target, your iron play is on point.

→ *Troubleshooting:* If you aren't hitting it as close as you'd like, you'll need to invest some time and energy to figure out why. Are you hitting poor shots? Are the poor results distance related? Or are they directional? Sourcing answers to these questions will help you isolate the variable that, if corrected, will improve performance. Alternatively, if you feel like you are hitting good shots, and not completing the task, make the task easier. See what happens when you extend the radius to seven or 10%.

3. CONTRA

→ *Objective:* To be a great iron player, you need to control all aspects of ball flight: distance, direction, trajectory, and curve. Contra challenges your ability to deliver functional outcomes while changing variables on each ball in random order Environment: Driving range with targets, or golf course.

→ *Tools:* Golf balls.

→ *Design:* Hit the following 11 shots to the same target in the specified order (P.S.: This refers to the famous cheat code to the legendary Nintendo game, Contra!!): High Shot, High Shot, Low Shot, Low Shot, Curve Left, Curve Right, Curve Left, Curve Right, One club less (swing hard), One club more (swing soft), Stock shot.

→ *Objective:* Just like previous challenge, your goal is to execute the shot as required AND have the ball finish within five percent of the shot distance, from the cup. As you go through the exercise, keep track of how many shots finish inside that 5% radius.

→ *Completion Cue:* If you're able to have more than 60% of your shots finish inside the radius, you are performing at a high level.

→ *Troubleshooting:* If you are missing the target radius, reverse engineer the reasons why. Are your misses due to direction or distance? You can either isolate these problems and work on them with the other drills, or relax the radius requirements to 7 or 10 percent.

SCRAMBLING

Clarifying Concept

I. GREENSIDE SOLID STRIKES

→ *Overview:* How do you deliver the club so you can avoid the common mishits—fat, thin, toe and heel shots? The answer to this questions represents the first step towards improving your short game performance. Around the greens, consistent contact is king. For finesse wedges, we need the club to strike the ball before the ground with a shallow brush of the turf in front of the ball.

→ *Environment:* Short Game Area, preferred short game wedge, no Target

→ *Tools:* Tees, towel

→ *Design:* Place a rolled up towel inside the ball parallel to the target line. The ball should be three inches ahead of the towel, and the, should be three inches inside the target line. Place a

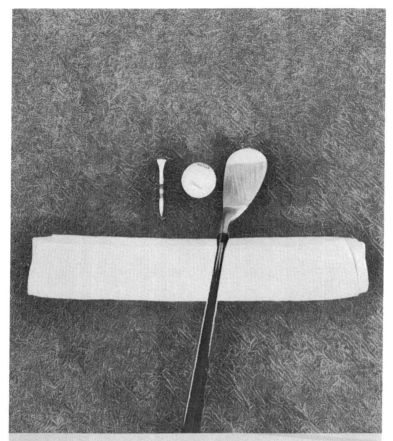

FOCUS ON MAKING SOLID, BALL-FIRST CONTACT, WHILE GENTLY
CLIPPING THE TEE AND MISSING THE TOWEL. THIS ENSURES YOU ARE
DELIVERING THE CLUB AT THE RIGHT ANGLE TO THE GROUND—AND TARGET.

tee horizontally on the ground a half inch in front of the ball.

→ *Objective:* The goal is to miss the towel and brush the tee in front of the ball, sending the ball and the tee airborne.

→ *Completion Cue:* If you can successfully strike the ball and front tee while avoiding the towel five times in a row with your favorite wedge, you're building a foundation for flush wedge shots.

→ *Troubleshooting:* Most wedge contact errors are a function of a poor setup. The biggest issue we see with our students is a too-strong grip, followed closely by the hands being set too far forward, the body closed, and the shoulders tilted at the sky. Check these elements of your setup in a mirror to identify possible areas for improvement that will produce a shallow brush of the turf in front of the ball.

2. GREENSIDE TRAJECTORY EXPLORATION

→ *Overview:* For the most part, the loft you deliver to the ball at impact is what determines the trajectory and spin of your shots. Additionally, the trajectory and spin of the shot will influence how much it rolls out, and ultimately, how far it goes. This task will help you start to learn to use the height of the shot as a means to control distance.

→ *Environment:* Short game area, preferred wedge, no target

→ *Tools:* None

→ *Design:* None

→ *Objective:* The goal isn't perfect execution. We want you to leave this task with a fundamental awareness of what goes into hitting shots of different heights—a mixture of club selection, ball position and face position at address. Hit ten shots with your preferred club in your normal set up and face position at address. Take note of the height at which the ball flies. Hit 10 more balls, but alter one of the three principles—club selection, setup or face position. Take note of what each ball does in comparison to what the previous 10 did.

→ *Completion Cue:* You can move on when you are able to hit six shots alternating between low, medium, and high trajectory by combining and/or manipulating the trajectory control elements.

→ *Troubleshooting:* Through trial and error, you'll likely come to experience some combination of setup elements that are dysfunctional. For example, a ball being played forward in your stance with your shoulders closed and tiled back. This predisposes you to hit behind the ball, excessively. Take note of what these are and move on. As a side note, if you're interested in escalating the level of difficulty, start with club selection as a trajectory modifier, then move on ball position, and then face alignment.

3. CONSTANT LANDING SPOT

→ *Overview:* Ball speed determines how far the ball goes. In the short game, that tends to fall on the shoulders of club selection (how much loft is applied to the ball), backswing length (how much speed is applied to the club), and the quality of the strike). This task will help you dial in those elements.

→ *Environment:* Short game area, preferred wedges no target

→ *Tools:* None

→ *Design:* None

→ *Objective:* This task is designed to help you develop an understanding of why the ball travels as far as it does, and how the force you use coupled with the club you pick makes it happen. Three things determine ball speed—club selection, backswing length and impact quality. Hit ten shots with your preferred club and normal setup and face alignment. Take note of the consistency at which the ball flies. Do the shots land in a similar place? Do they fly with the same trajectory? Hit ten more balls, but change one of the three principles—either club selection, backswing length or impact quality. Try to make those balls land at the same target spot as your initial ten.

→ *Completion Cue:* If you can successfully land 50% of the shots from your second 10 balls within two club lengths of the first 10 shots, you are ready to start develop the skill of varying the carry by manipulating the determining factors of distance.

→ *Troubleshooting:* Major distance control errors are most often caused by faulty contact. If you are struggling with this, dial down the difficulty of the task, and re-visit the solid contact exercise. It can also help to make sure that your set-up is on point.

Diversifying Skill Set

I. VARIED TRAJECTORY SOLID STRIKES

→ *Overview:* Players are often confident in hitting one type of shot solid, but you're going to encounter variety of shots throughout a round. You need the tools to be able to hit a variety of shots to solve a variety of scenarios.

→ *Environment:* Short game area, preferred wedge, one target

→ *Tools:* Tees, golf towel

→ *Design:* Place a rolled up towel inside the ball parallel to the target line. The ball should be three inches ahead of the towel, and the towel should be three inches inside the target line. Place a tee horizontally on the ground a half inch in front of the ball.

→ *Objective:* The goal is to miss the towel and brush the tee in front of the ball, sending the ball and the tee airborne. Unlike the first solid contact task, this time you are required to vary the trajectory of these shots. If you normally struggle striking your higher trajectory shots solid, we want you to hone in on that opportunity for improvement. Alternating between mid, high, and low trajectories. Review the trajectory exploration in the previous task as a refresher for how to modify trajectory and use this task to make sure you can produce solid strikes for all the shots.

→ *Completion Cue:* If you can successfully strike the ball and front tee while avoiding the towel for four of five low shots, four of five mid-height shots, and four of five high shots with your favorite wedge, you've developed a clear concept for what is needed to strike solid iron shots for each of the trajectories.

→ *Troubleshooting:* If you're struggling to complete the drill, its best to dial down the difficulty and return to the previous task. The most common errors come from poor contact, as a result of a bad setup. Check the setup elements from the first task for a review.

2. LANDING ZONE LEAPFROG

→ *Overview:* The best short game practitioners are able to make subtle changes to shot trajectory and distance to suit the situation they face. This task will encourage you to develop those skills.

→ *Environment:* Short game area, preferred wedges, hole

→ *Tools:* Ball marker

→ *Design:* Select an area that is about five to ten yards from the green, and where there is approximately 30 feet between the front of the green and the hole.

→ *Objective:* Your goal is to land each ball progressively farther than the shot prior, while having each ball finish within nine feet of the hole. Hit your first shot and mark the spot where it landed with the ball marker. Your next ball must fly past that spot, and finish within nine feet of the hole. Repeat this process until you run out of space.

→ *Completion Cue:* If you can successfully hit five shots following this distance ladder and have each finish within nine feet, that is evidence you have increased the diversity of your skill.

→ *Troubleshooting:* When people struggle with this task, it is usually because they lack control of how much force they apply to the club, and change the trajectory too drastically. If you are struggling, go back to the trajectory and force control exercises in clarify concept to gain more command over each element.

3. CLUB SELECTION KNOCKOUT

→ *Overview:* "Touch" tends to be a mystical word in golf, but it is simply a measure of your ability to regulate force. Being able to control how far the ball travels—in this case, being able to hit the shot the same distance with a variety of clubs—epitomizes that skill. It's a handy one to know.

→ *Environment:* Short game area, three short game clubs, target

→ *Tools:* None

→ *Design:* Select a spot around the green that is roughly five to ten yards from the green. From this spot, you should have at least 20 feet between you and the hole.

→ *Task Objective:* Your goal is to get the ball within nine feet of the hole using three different clubs. Hit your first ball using one club. If it finishes within the required proximity to target, change clubs. If not, repeat until it finishes inside the required distance. Repeat until all clubs are "knocked out."

→ *Completion Cue:* If you're able to hit three balls inside the required distance to the target within four shots, you've demonstrated the capability to regulate force through the bag and have a greater sense of touch.

→ *Troubleshooting:* If you're struggling, it is likely a function of awareness and shot comfort. You're being asked to play a shot in a way you wouldn't normally hit it. Try going back to the touch explorations in clarify concept and work through different combinations of the principles that determine force to heighten your awareness.

Building Belief

I. AROUND THE WORLD

→ *Overview:* Through the first two Scrambling Solid Strike stations, you've grown your ability and confidence to produce solid strikes within a stable environment. But you also have to be able to make the necessary modifications to produce solid strikes from a variety of lies. So when you encounter a tough lie, we want you to be able reference back to your experience in training this ability from a variety of conditions and approach the shot with a sense of 'I-can-do-it-ness.'

→ *Environment:* Short game area, preferred wedges, multiple targets

→ *Tools:* Tees, golf towel

→ *Design:* Pick six locations around the green, each with a slightly different lie. Look for uphill/downhill lies, ball above and below your feet, and a variety of different grass conditions—deep, fluffy, tight, bare.

→ *Task Objective:* Start at the first location and attempt to make the necessary modification to produce a solid strike from that lie and get the ball to finish within a flagstick of the hole. Once you are able to do this, move on to the next location. Repeat, moving on to each lie until you've hit a successful shot from each location.

→ *Completion Cue:* You graduate from this task when you can go "around the world" and play shots from all six locations successfully in one attempt.

→ *Troubleshooting:* If you're struggling to hit a solid shot from a certain lie, remember: the lie will dictate how steeply or shallowly you should be delivering the clubhead. Spend some time reflecting on which shots troubled you the most, and consider if they require a steep or shallow angle of attack. For example, a ball sitting down in deep rough requires a steeper angle of attack than a tight lie in the fairway. Experiment with changes in your setup or swing that would allow you to optimize your angle of attack for any shot you face.

2. VARIABLE TRAJECTORY KNOCKOUT

→ *Overview:* You will inevitably face a situation that requires a short game shot with your less-than-favorite trajectory. Seeing yourself be successful using different shot heights to hit it close in a variety of conditions is a key component of improving your performance around the greens—and building belief in your short game.

→ *Environment:* Short game area, preferred wedge

→ *Tools:* Ball markers

→ *Design:* Identify four locations around the green—two in the fairway and two in the rough. At least one shot should be from a downhill lie, and another should be uphill.

→ *Objective:* Your goal is to hit two shots, each with different trajectories, within a flagstick length of the hole from each of the four locations using your one wedge. Starting at your first location, place two ball markers on the green to identify your two landing spots. Once you get the ball within a flagstick length while landing within three feet of your first ball marker, you may progress to the next ball marker. Repeat this process for each ball marker at each location.

→ *Completion Cue:* When you can do this task successfully 50 percent of the time, you'll know that you've got the skill to get any ball close to the hole.

→ *Troubleshooting:* If you're having trouble with a specific shot, start by taking away the proximity requirement. Pare down the environment and watch intently how the ball reacts when it hits the ground. Are you hitting your spot, but the ball isn't stopping where you want it to? Consider what that means: it means that you're simply judging the shot incorrectly. The outcomes is a function of either selecting the wrong landing spot or hitting the shot too high or too low. That said, if you can't hit the landing spot, go back to some of the contact or distance control tasks from the diversify skill section.

3. VARIABLE CLUB KNOCKOUT

→ *Overview:* Confidence comes from knowing you have a variety of shots at your disposal—and that you are equipped for all scenarios. This task will give you regular confirmation in practice that you are developing the ability to not only adapt to variability, but also to excel. While similar to the previous drill, this task challenges your ability to hit multiple shots the same distance while changing the trajectory, and club used, on each shot.

→ *Environment:* Short game area, two clubs

→ *Tools:* Ball markers

→ *Design:* As in the previous task, identify four locations around the green—two in the fairway, two in the rough and with a variety of lies.

→ *Task Objective:* Your goal is to hit two shots, each with a different landing spot and different club, within a flagstick length of the hole from each of the four locations. Starting at your first location, place two ball markers on the green to identify your two landing spots. Once you get the ball within a flagstick length while landing within three feet of your first ball marker, you can progress to the next ball marker and club. Repeat this process for each ball marker at each location.

→ *Completion Cue:* Once you're able to achieve a 50% success rate, you'll know that you've got the skill to get any ball close to the hole.

→ *Troubleshooting:* Follow the same troubleshooting advice from the previous task. If you struggle, take away the proximity requirement and examine why your shots aren't doing what you expect. Are the errors judgement based (ie: wrong trajectory) or performance based (ie: poor contact)? If necessary, call an audible and train the skill that is causing the gap.

Transferring Skill

I. SCORING SPIRAL

→ *Overview:* This task provides you with an opportunity to put all of your short game skills together in a very golf-like environment. Training this way improves the degree to which the skills transfer to the course.

→ *Environment:* Short game clubs, practice green complex

→ *Tools:* None

→ *Design:* Choose five different shots around the green, varying them from easy to hard and picking different lies in the fairway, rough, and/or sand. Starting at one location, play your chip, pitch, or sand shot onto the green. If you hole your putt and successfully get up and down, move on to the next location. If you miss, repeat the hole. Complete this process until you get the ball up and down from the final location. If, for example, you fail to get the ball up and down at the third location, you only go back one spot—not all the way to the beginning.

→ *Objective:* You're enhancing your ability to get up and down from a variety of locations both by working on technique and simulating the pressure that comes in real scenarios.

→ *Completion Cue:* If you're getting the ball up and down half the time and are able to complete the task, you're operating at an optimum level and the task is appropriately challenging.

→ *Troubleshooting:* Isolate the specific shot that is causing the most problems—lie, location, trajectory—and go back to the appropriate task and review.

2. PAR-BIRDIE-BOGEY SHORT GAME

→ *Overview:* This task provides you with an opportunity to put all of your short game skills together in an authentic environment, and with the pressure of achieving a recognizable score.

→ *Environment:* Short game clubs, green

→ *Tools:* None

→ *Design:* Choose nine different shots around the green—three "easy" shots, three "moderate" shots, and three "hard" shots. All of the easy shots will require you to get up and down for bogey. The moderate shots will require you to get up and down for par, and the hard shots will require you to get up and down for birdie.

→ *Objective:* Your goal is to score as low as possible. The lower you score, the more adaptable your short game is, and the greater the chance for success during play.

→ *Completion Cue:* If you're able to score +3 or better, your short game is very strong. If you're struggling to shoot +5, consider

why. Distance? Shot selection? Trajectory?

→ *Troubleshooting:* If the struggle persists, decrease the difficulty by isolating the specific element of the performance that you feel is off.

3. 2-SHAPE WORSE BALL

→ *Overview:* This task requires massive amounts of creativity and adaptability as it forces you to utilize two different shot types from each location. To further challenge you, you have to putt out from the 'Worse Ball' location.

→ *Environment:* Chipping green or on-course green complex

→ *Tools:* Multiple short game clubs

→ *Design:* From nine different locations within 30 yards of the green, play two balls—with the added challenge that you must play two different types of shots and clearly state the adaptation you'll make in club selection, landing zone or trajectory for each shot—and putt out from the ball that ended up farthest from the hole.

→ *Objective:* Your goal is to score as low as possible. The lower you score, the more adaptable your short game is, and the greater the chance for success during play.

→ *Completion Cue:* This tasks presents a very high degree of difficulty. Create a benchmark score when you complete the game for the first time. This represents your personal best and you should strive to match or improve upon that score with each attempt.

→ *Troubleshooting:* Isolate the specific shot that is causing the most problems—lie, location, trajectory—and go back to the appropriate task and review.

PUTTING

Clarifying Concept

I. 2-BALL TEST

→ *Overview:* Where the ball starts in largely determined by the angle of the face at impact. Here, you'll get feedback on where your start line tendencies are—which is the first priority in improving your putting.

→ *Environment:* Putting green, putter, no target

→ *Tools:* Two balls

→ *Design:* Place two balls right next to each other, lined up perpendicular to the target line. Both balls should be touching the face of the putter.

→ *Objective:* The goal of the task is to take some strokes while returning the putter face square at impact. You will be able to tell if you did this by the finishing position of the balls relative to each other. If the outside ball travels further, it is an indication that the putter face was closed at impact—and vice versa for an open face.

→ *Completion Cue:* If you can get both balls to finish within close proximity five times in a row, you are on the right track.

→ *Troubleshooting:* A number of factors can contribute to an inability to return a square putter face—from poor alignment to incorrect movement of the hands through stroke. If you are struggling, start by looking at where you are aiming your putter at address. Oftentimes, a misaligned putter can cause you to make large variations in clubface to get the ball near to the target. If the putter face is aimed close to your intended line, and the ball isn't going there, you'll need to take a closer look at your mechanics (grip, ball position, body alignment).

ENSURE THAT BOTH BALLS ARE TOUCHING THE PUTTER AT ADDRESS.
FOCUS ON GETTING THE BALLS TO FINISH AS CLOSE TO ONE ANOTHER AS
POSSIBLE. THIS WILL HELP YOU DEVELOP MORE CONTROL OF THE CLUB FACE.

2. BLIND FROG

→ *Overview:* Speed is controlled mostly by the length of your stroke and the acceleration of the putter through impact. To be a great putter you need to control these elements with precision and consistency. This exercise provides you with a way to calibrate your speed, and enhance your touch, on a daily basis.

→ *Environment:* Putting green, putter, no target

→ *Tools:* Ball marker, three tees, three balls

→ *Design:* Place a tee in the ground at your starting location, and

another in the green ten feet away. Stick a third tee 30 feet away, which creates a 20-foot long zone between the two far tees.

→ *Objective:* The goal is to roll the first ball just past the second tee, and each subsequent ball within a putter length past the previous putt. Before looking up to see if you were successful, attempt to guess while the ball is still rolling where it will finish in relation to your intended outcome. The guessing element is a critical step in the task because it makes you to calibrate your feel immediately following each trial.

→ *Completion Cue:* If you can place seven balls in succession within your the second and third tee, you can move on.

→ *Troubleshooting:* If you're struggling, the first place to look would be the rate of acceleration through impact. Use a verbal counting method, like 'tic-toc' or '1 and 2' while you hit the putts to help you determine if the through-stroke is too fast or forceful. Smoothing out the acceleration or coasting the putter through impact are a helpful mechanisms for improving touch.

3. STRAIGHT PUTT SEARCH

→ *Overview:* The ball breaks because of slope. Being able to find straight putts and understand the degree to which slope effects putts is a key skill to develop as you improve your green-reading.

→ *Environment:* Putting green, hole

→ *Tools:* Ten balls.

→ *Design:* Place ten balls in a six-foot circle around a hole. Two of these putts are likely to be straight. Walk around each ball. As you walk, be aware of how the terrain shifts under your feet. When you can identify the point at which the slope starts to go in the opposite direction, you've discovered the straight putt.

→ *Objective:* The goal of this task is to successfully identify the

STRAIGHT PUTT SEARCH

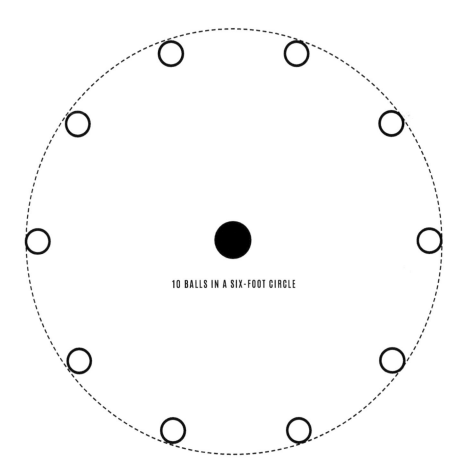

10 BALLS IN A SIX-FOOT CIRCLE

SURROUND THE HOLE WITH TEES OR COINS. DO YOU BEST
TO IDENTIFY THE STRAIGHT PUTTS AROUND THE HOLE.

straight putt(s) around a hole. After you think you've got the straight putt(s), go ahead and hit them and see what happens. From there, do your best to read the other putts and hole them out too. As you go through the exercise, take note of whether your intended read was correct. Was one type of putt, for example left to right, more difficult than others?

→ *Completion Cue:* If you are able to hole half of your six footers, that is an indication your ability to read putts—and get the ball started on your intended line—is pretty good.

→ *Troubleshooting:* For players struggling to complete this task, use a tee and punch a small hole in the ground 12" ahead of your ball on your intended line. If your ball is consistently rolling over the dot, this would indicate a read error. If your ball is missing the dot, go back to the previous drill and develop more control of the putter face through impact.

Diversifying Skill Set

I. FACE ERROR AMPLIFICATION

→ *Overview:* To be a good putter, you need to deliver the face square to the intended line consistently. To do that, you have to have an awareness of where the face is throughout the stroke. Creating a spectrum with two extremes lets you create a sensation that you can reference. You can find optimal by experiencing opposites.

→ *Environment:* Putting green, putter, hole

→ *Tools:* Three balls, tees

→ *Design:* Find a fairly straight putt (you can do this now!). Create a gate on the target line that is two balls wide and about two feet ahead of the ball.

→ *Objective:* The goal of the task is to get three balls in a row through the gate using three different strokes. The first one

CREATE A GATE ON THE TARGET LINE WITH TWO TEES. THE GATES
SHOULD BE TWO BALLS WIDE AND ABOUT TWO FEET AHEAD OF THE BALL.

should be an exaggerated over-rotation of the face going back. The second should be an exaggerated under-rotation of the face going back, and the third should be an optimal middle ground. Some players are afraid this drill will "ruin" their stroke, but research shows that short spurts of error amplification like this are great for enhancing your awareness.

→ *Completion Cue:* If you can get three in a row through the gate with those variable patterns three times, you'll have developed

a heightened sense of where the face is, and be on your way to better putting.

→ *Troubleshooting:* This task is designed to produce some degree of failure, as we are activity amplifying errors in order to better locate optimum. Consequently, there really is no need to get caught up in the result. However, if you are finding hard to achieve the middle ground—the optimal face rotation—dial it back and revert to the 2 ball drill from clarify concept.

2. 8-BALL CHALLENGE

→ *Overview:* Every putt you encounter is different—in length, break, speed, etc. As such, you have to have have a system for calibrating the power you put into your stroke for a variety of distances.
→ *Environment:* Putting green, putter one hole with decent amount of break.
→ *Tools:* Three tees, eight golf balls marked 1-8
→ *Design:* Place a tee in the ground at you starting location, another ten feet away, and the third 30 feet away from the starting location—creating a 20-foot long zone between the far tees.
→ *Objective:* Your goal is to get all eight balls within the designated zone, but there's a twist. You have to get the numbered balls in order, from 1 to 8. Randomly choose a ball from your pile of numbered balls and putt it where you think it will need to be within your zone to put you in the best position to putt the remaining balls in order. For example, if your first ball is the 7 ball, you need to putt it to the end of the zone while still leaving enough room between the long boundary and the 7 ball for you to fit the 8 ball between. There is some strategy and massive amount of touch required to complete this drill successfully and end up with all eight balls in order.

8-BALL CHALLENGE

STRIVE TO ACHIEVE EQUAL
SPACING BETWEEN EACH
BALL. THIS EPITOMIZES
THE ABILITY TO CONTROL
SPEED OVER A BROAD RANGE
OF DISTANCES.

→ *Completion Cue:* Once all the balls are ordered 1-8, within the zone, you are free to move on to a different task.

→ *Troubleshooting:* If you are struggling to achieve the desired outcome, instead of choosing the balls randomly, complete the drill by going in order 1-8. If you still struggle to complete, reduce the number of golf balls. As you achieve success with fewer balls, start integrating more, as this will demand you to more precisely regulate force. If reducing the number of balls doesn't help, go back to the exercise in clarify concept.

3. THREE TEE SPEED DRILL

→ *Overview:* For any given breaking putt, there are a variety of speed and line combinations that you can choose. As you practice all of the different combinations, you start to develop greater touch. You also begin to assimilate information applicable for all the green conditions that you'll encounter across different courses.

→ *Environment:* Putting green, putter, one hole with decent amount of break

→ *Tools:* Three tees, three golf balls

→ *Design:* Put three tees in the inner edge of the hole. The first tee denotes where the ball will enter the cup when hit with firmer than normal speed. The second tee marks the point at which the ball will go in the hole when hit with normal speed. The third tee represents the point at which the ball will enter the cup when hit with softer than normal speed.

→ *Objective:* The goal is to roll a ball into the hole at three different speeds, all from six feet away. Use the tees inside the cup as reference for the intended line and entry point for each attempt. For the first putt, use the straightest line and hit it firm enough to enter over the first tee. Continue alternating between the three entry points, modifying your speed as you roll in putts over each of your three designated entry points.

→ *Completion Cue:* If you can make all three putts in four attempts from six feet, that serves to tell you that you can move on.

→ *Troubleshooting:* If you are having trouble identifying three different entry locations for the putt, choose a putt with more break.

Building Belief

1. RANDOM DOT DRILL

→ *Overview:* With this task, you are just attempting to confirm your ability to start putts on line from any slope you encounter. Players are often unaware of start line issues that could occur on sloping putts. For example, a player may have a tendency to start right-to-left putts too high, playing too much break. Being aware of these tendencies and using this task to confirm that you are starting ALL putts on line can provide a crucial boost of confidence on the greens.

→ *Environment:* Putting green, putter, hole with heavy slope near it

→ *Tools:* Sharpie, ball

→ *Design:* Alternate between right to left and left to right putts, anywhere between 4-12 feet in length. Place a tee outside the hole where you think the ball needs to start for it to go in. Using your sharpie, make a small dot on the green, 12 inches ahead of your ball, on that line. Roll the ball over the dot.

→ *Objective:* The goal is to grow your awareness for any start line tendencies on breaking putts while confirming your proficiency in starting putts on line. While there is obviously a green-reading element to the task, our focus here is on start line. So rather

than be overly concerned with making the putts, just focus your attention on whether the putts are starting on line. As you evaluate your ability to do this, take time to reflect on each attempt, so you can become more aware of any patterns in your misses and use that feedback to inform future trials.

→ *Completion Cue:* Once you're able to hit five putts in a row so that they roll over the dot, you're showing you're able to keep the ball starting on line over a variety of different putts.

→ *Troubleshooting:* If you're struggling, notice which putts you are struggling with. Once identified, spend a bit more time repeating this task on that type of putt.

2. PUTTING PAR-5

→ *Overview:* This task is designed to build belief in your ability to control speed from some critical putting distances. Putts from four to seven feet are crucial. Making them is often the difference between an OK round and a great one. Similarly, lagging long putts to makeable range is equally critical to scoring.

→ *Environment:* Putting green, putter

→ *Tools:* None

→ *Design:* Pick a hole on the practice green and set balls four, seven and 30 feet away.

→ *Objective:* You're trying to build your ability to control speed from these crucial distances while testing that ability from a variety of locations. The goal is to hole out the four footer, seven footer and 30-footer in five shots or less. This will obviously require a make (likely from the first two locations) while two putting the others.

→ *Completion Cue:* Once you successfully hole out all three putts in five putts or less from six different locations—preferably

CREATE A SMALL DOT ON THE GREEN APPROXIMATELY 12-18 INCHES
AHEAD OF YOUR BALL ON YOUR INTENDED LINE. FOCUS ON HAVING THE
BALL ROLL OVER THE DOT ON ITS WAY TO THE HOLE.

alternating between downhill, uphill, and sidehill—you're ready to move on.

→ *Troubleshooting:* If you're struggling, go back to the previous tasks that focus on developing your ability to control your speed on the greens.

3. 9-HOLE GREEN READING TEST

→ *Overview:* This task is designed to help raise your awareness of your green reading skills and tendencies. By being structured in a way that provides you with clear feedback on whether or not the read was correct, you get evidence of correctness or an understanding of your error patterns. Both points of information help you be more confident on the course. If this task is completed successfully, you can approach putts with total trust in your ability to read the greens correctly and focus on just getting the ball started on your line.

→ *Environment:* Putting green, putter

→ *Tools:* Tee, sharpie, ball

→ *Design:* Choose nine putts of different lengths and slopes. As with the random dot drill, place a tee outside the hole where you think the ball needs to start for it to go in. Using your sharpie, make a small dot on the green, 12 inches ahead of your ball and on the line. Roll the ball over the dot. Do your best to have your uphill putts finish two feet past, and your downhill putts finish one foot past. Keeping this as a constant goal throughout the process will help you isolate the green-reading aspect of the task—which makes sure you don't confuse speed or line errors with green-reading errors.

→ *Objective:* The objective is to grow your awareness for any start line tendencies on breaking putts while confirming your proficiency in starting putts on line. If the ball rolls over the dot and into the hole, you know you made a good stroke and had the correct read. If it rolls over the dot and misses the hole, you know that the read was incorrect. If it misses the dot and goes in, you know you manipulated the face and that your intended line wasn't what it actually was. This process will help you identify any tendencies—good and bad—you have in your aim and start line.

→ *Completion Cue:* If you're able to consistently get the ball on line at your intended target AND your intended target is correct, as evidenced by makes and lip-outs, you can feel good about your green reading.

→ *Troubleshooting:* If you're struggling, notice which element is most difficult—either green reading or start line control. After diagnosing, train that skill in isolation to build your confidence and proficiency in it.

Transferring Skill

I. PAR 15 PUTTING

→ *Overview:* This task provides you with a way to test the marriage of your putting skills under a variety of conditions and in a very random order —just like golf.

→ *Environment:* Putting green, putter

→ *Tools:* Putter

→ *Design:* Hit one putt from each of the following distances: three, five, seven, nine, 12, 12, 15, 21, 27 and 36 feet. Make sure you have a variety of different breaks and slopes, and aren't repeating lines.

→ *Objective:* You're trying to score as low as possible. The lower you score, the more adept you are at reading greens and matching those reads with appropriate speed.

→ *Completion Cue:* If you're able to score 14 or better, it signals to you that your putting is strong. If you're struggling to beat 16, consider why. Are your reads off? Speed? Not starting the ball on line?

→ *Troubleshooting:* Isolate your issues. Are you having trouble with distance on the longer putts? Starting the ball on the right line? Reading? When you have identified your issue, work on it specifically with one of the previous tasks.

2. PAR-BIRDIE-BOGEY PUTTING

→ *Overview:* This task provides you with a high level of challenge while layering on elements of luck and pressure that you are sure to encounter out on the course.

→ *Environment:* Putting green, putter

→ *Tools:* Putter, nine balls (three marked "+1," three marked "0" and three marked "-1" in sharpie

→ *Design:* Pick a hole and toss up the balls to randomly distribute them between three and 15 feet from the hole. Working your way from farthest to closest to the hole, putt all nine putts keeping track of your score. Balls marked with +1 are for bogey, balls marked with -1 are for birdie, and balls marked with 0 are for par.

→ *Objective:* Your goal is to score as low as possible. Compete against others or against your personal best to finish with the lowest score.

→ *Completion Cue:* If you're able to score +1 or better, your putting is very strong. If you're struggling to shoot +4, consider why. Distance? Shot selection? Trajectory?

→ *Troubleshooting:* If the struggle persists, decrease the difficulty by isolating the specific element of the performance that you feel is off.

3. RAT RACE

→ *Overview:* This task is another progression task that requires you to hole out a succession of short to mid range putts. Your ability to hole these length putts will often separate mediocre rounds from great ones.

→ *Environment:* Putting Green

→ *Tools:* Putter, 10 Balls

→ *Design:* Place 10 balls around the hole at random distances from four to 12 feet from the hole.

→ *Objective:* Select a putt to start from. The goal is to make it around, holing out all 10 balls. Make the first putt to advance to the next location. If you miss a putt three times in a row, move back to the previous location.

→ *Completion Cue:* You've completed the task when you have made it to the final location and holed out from there. This is a great game to play against an opponent in a race to be the first to hole out from all 10 locations.

→ *Troubleshooting:* This tasks is designed to be very "golf-like," simulating the kind of variety and pressure you encounter on the course. To complete the tasks, you're required to successfully make a read, control start line, and speed. If you are struggling, you need to isolate which of those components is the biggest reason for missed putts. Decide which area is holding you back and address it with the appropriate task provided earlier in the Putting Practice Plan.

CHAPTER 5

THE ATTITUDE: WHAT DOES A SUPER-LEARNER LOOK LIKE?

OUR GOAL WITH THIS BOOK has been to give you a concrete plan for what to go out and actually *do* in your quest to get better.

But it would be coaching malpractice if we didn't have a conversation about the common mental traits and mindsets that make the process of improvement more productive and more rewarding.

In some ways, you're already self-selecting as a player with the right mindset—because you recognize that you want to improve, and you've taken the step of seeking out coaching from us in this book.

But there's more to the ultimate learner's mindset than just wanting to shoot better scores. The motivation behind that desire goes a long way toward predicting how successful a player is ultimately going to be in his or her search.

What drives you?

Do you want to get better because of the satisfaction of building toward mastery in something? That's classic *internal motivation*. Or are you more interested in getting better so that you can beat the guys you play with, or qualify for the first flight of the club championship? That's classic *external motivation*.

Looking back through the years of work we've been doing

with our students, the most satisfying relationships we've had—and the best results—have come from players with a strong sense of internal motivation. They were most interested in mastering the skill—which ultimately produced better scores.

That isn't a blanket condemnation of external motivation. If you're committed to the process of learning and are willing to put in the time, an external goal like breaking a certain scoring barrier can work. In fact, researchers have discovered that most successful Olympians achieve a nice balance of both internal and external motivation. It's just harder to sustain over the long haul if you're relying exclusively on external motivation to drive you forward.

Whichever motivation fuel you have, you can make the conscious decision to model the "super-learner" traits we're going to talk about below, and practice the tactics that will make you a more receptive learner—whether you're absorbing information from a book or taking lessons live from an instructor.

We can't stress this enough. These traits contribute to a learning mindset that will ultimately determine your success. They're the most common threads linking our most successful students. The correlation between positive learning mindsets and success is too significant to be ignored. Take advantage of it and you can dramatically improve your training.

SUPER-LEARNER TRAITS

Conscientiousness

THE VALUE IN THIS TRAIT is the same for adults as it was when you were in kindergarten. A conscientious person is somebody who puts their full effort and attention into what they're doing. It means you try. Plenty of golfers are interested in getting better, but only to the extent that they'll look for a quick-fix solution. The minute there is any complexity or adversity, they move on to the next thing.

Our favorite students are the ones who get a piece of homework to do before the next lesson and come back having completed it fully and precisely. Less conscientious players are easily distracted, and are usually quick with reasons why they couldn't take the next step in their practice or development. They aren't fully committed to the improvement process.

Curiosity

LEARNING GOLF (or any other complex skill) isn't just about following a checklist of data points. The most engaging and exciting learning process is the one where the student and teacher are both fully invested in what is happening, and are working together on the hunt for the best solution. The best students are always curious about the "why" questions, not just the "how" ones. Why does a certain exercise work in ingraining habits, while another one doesn't? What happens if we combine elements of one routine with the elements of another one? So many players go an entire career struggling with the same mistakes because they see a bad shot and have no idea why it happened. The curious player asks questions that demystify their common mistakes, and sends them on a path toward improvement. They know the "why," which leads them to the "how."

Solution Orientation

Watch a practice session with a super-learner and you'll see a lot of things that are different than the "standard" lesson. One that stands out is the active learner's relationship with "failure." A receptive, curious player will hit a really bad shot and be intrigued by it. Why did that happen? What did I do differently, and how do I fix it? Other players tend to let emotion rule the moment. They hit some bad shots and get angry. Maybe they slam a club, or put the offending club away and hit something else. None of that addresses the real issue— finding a solution to the ball-flight problem at hand.

Tenacity

Golf is incredibly frustrating—even for the best players. We aren't robots, and performance changes from day to day. That's especially true when you've been put off balance during a learning process. The best students are determined to work through short-term setbacks because they see the bigger picture. Hitting some bad shots for a few days? It's a blip on the screen, and doesn't mean you aren't trending in the right direction overall. And then there's just the raw effort that comes with mastering any skill. You can't read or hack your way into mastery. It takes directed practice and time. Players willing and happy to put in the work are almost always going to be in better position than ones that aren't.

Self-Compassion

A GAIN, WE AREN'T MACHINES. You can't do everything per-fectly, and things don't always go according to plan. That's the reality, and if you anticipate something different, you're going to be frustrated. The best learners understand how to keep things in perspective, and how to put setbacks in the proper context. This is where your *self-talk* comes in. It's just what it sounds like. Self-talk is the inner conversation you're having with yourself as you do something. If you hit a bad shot and immediately think about how terrible you are and how you're never going to break 90, that's a fine example of neg-ative self-talk.

Our friends Pia and Lynn at Vision54 describe the storage of positive memories as the mechanics of building confidence. The inverse is also true. When you're unforgiving during the process of improvement, you not only limit your rate of im-provement but you extinguish the confidence and motivation you need to fight through the inevitable failures you'll encoun-ter along the way.

We're obviously not saying emotions have no part in golf, or demanding that you train yourself to be completely blank when you make a mistake. But developing the ability to feel that anger or disappointment and then let it dissipate is an incredibly important skill. It starts with changing around your self-talk to reinforce objective, calming elements—not self-destructive ones.

Which player do you think is going to have the best chance at hitting the next shot great? The one who says he or she can't wait to take on the challenge to get up and down from that super tough spot? Or the one who is still beating himself

or herself up for making the bad swing that put the ball in the bad spot in the first place?

WHICH ONE ARE YOU?	
SOLUTION=ORIENTED	DEFEATIST/FATALISTIC
CURIOUS TO SELF DISCOVER	COMPLIANT TO COACH
ACTIVE PARTICIPANT OF LEARNING	PASSIVE RECIPIENT OF INSTRUCTION
CONSCIENTIOUS	CARELESS
SELF COMPASSION	SELF-CRITICAL
FOLLOWS A PLAN	REACTIVE SEARCHING

SUPER-LEARNER TACTICS

IDENTIFYING TRAITS is the first step in the process. Coming up with concrete actions that will emphasize those traits is the critical step. Even if you don't believe you truly have some of the traits described above, you can get a lot of the benefit of them simply by committing to using some of these tactics.

Meticulous Practice

SOMETHING ABOUT THE DRIVING RANGES turns so many players into metronomes. They get a giant bucket of balls and rifle through them as fast as possible, aiming for the same target—or, worse, at no target. They might try some new things here or there, but if it doesn't work they try something else right away—and never learn anything about the real issue.

On the other hand, a meticulous practicer comes to the range with a very specific idea of what he or she wants to accomplish and plan to do it. The plan isn't derailed by a couple of bad shots, and isn't dependent on whether somebody feels like doing it or not. It's an assignment, just like homework was in junior high. And the students who did the homework got better grades.

It's impossible to stress how big this tactic is in the scheme of things. If you didn't do *anything* else besides read this book and follow the basic instructions for setting up a practice plan meticulously, you'd be guaranteeing yourself improvement in your game. But it's something most players never do!

Reflection

HOW DO YOU KNOW if you're headed in the right direction with your practice and game development? That comes from spending time away from the active practice field thinking and reflecting on what you're doing. It makes sense intuitively. If you aren't aware of what you're doing and where you stand, how are you going to know if you need to make any adjustments to your practice program.

Everything we're about is trying to get away from mindlessly beating balls and doing things the same way because you've always done it that way. It starts with a plan, and it works because you're conscious of the structure of that plan both while you're practicing and in between sessions and rounds.

If something is working when you're out on the course? Acknowledging that and thinking about how to grow it into all parts of your game is extremely valuable. It's just as true for situations where you don't perform your best. Reflecting on the "why" gives you fuel for your practice sessions and the work you need to do to reach your goals.

Goal-Setting

WHICH LEADS US into that exact subject—setting goals. It's a process that gets written off by many players, or seen as trivial and superficial. But if you don't set tangible goals for yourself, you're robbing yourself of a powerful motivational tool. "Saving some money" isn't the same as "Saving $5,000." "Lose some weight" isn't the same as "Lose 20 pounds." When you attach specificity to the goal, you're giving yourself a benchmark.

The goals don't have to have anything to do with shooting

a score—which would make them external instead of internal. They can be totally based on skill mastery. Maybe you're using a TrackMan when you have a lesson. You can challenge yourself to achieve a certain score on TrackMan's diagnostic Combine game by a certain time period. If you achieve it, you've been able to pull together a variety of different skills and turn them into specific shots.

Measuring

WITHOUT A WAY OF MEASURING your progress, like the Track-Man combine, you won't know if you're progressing, and how much. ShotLink is an awesome tool on the PGA Tour, because it gives players there every piece of information they could ever want about the quality of shots they hit in tournaments. It also reveals very clearly where they need to spend time on their games.

You probably don't have a person following you around to measure every shot you hit, but you can do a decent approximation of it yourself, just using a rangefinder and your scorecard. Keeping track of the basics like fairways hit, greens hit and number of putts is a good start, but when you expend it to measure how far you hit each tee shot with driver, how far you have into each hole, and the distance of each first putt, you're giving yourself a full scouting report on what situations you end up in the most often when you play.

If you're hitting a lot of drivers off the tee and missing a lot of them right—and leaving yourself with plenty of 175-yard shots into greens—you're foolish if you don't figure out a way (at least) to hit those shots a little better. Why wouldn't you want to know that kind of stuff if it was relatively easy to find it out?

The beauty of this game is that nothing is set in stone. You don't have to be tomorrow the player you were last week. By knowing what you need to do, and the best way to do it, you can take the small steps that translate into better scores.

You can master the habit of improvement. And that's something that you can use not just in your golf life, but in your real life.

SUPER-LEARNER TRAITS	LOUSY-LEARNER TRAITS
FOCUSED & COMMITTED	SCATTERED & REACTIVE
CURIOUS	COMPLIANT
ACTIVE PARTICIPANT	PASSIVE RECIPIENT
EXCITED TO LEARN	FEAR CHANGE
POSITIVE SELF-TALK	SELF-CRITICAL
DISCIPLINED	UNDISCIPLINED
REFLECTIVE	MINDLESS

ACKNOWLEDGMENTS

L IKE SO MANY OTHERS, I've always aspired to one day shift from consumer to creator—from an avid reader of so many books that have made a meaningful impact on me to an author. After starting the process and then ultimately stalling a few times, I eventually arrived at a startling realization— writing a book is hard. Without the generosity and guidance of a few very special people, the goal would have likely remained unrealized.

First, and perhaps most obviously—Matt Wilson. An unbelievable writing partner and friend. If you read something in this book or our blog that made you pause and marvel at its insight—Matt probably came up with the idea. He's really smart. We've traveled a fun road together, often stretching beyond what we thought we could accomplish, leaning on each other for the encouragement and motivation to remain bold in our ambitions and accountable in our actions.

Even when combining our efforts towards this book, we relied heavily on a few special mentors to help guide us along the process. James Sieckmann has provided endless advice and altruism to both of us, even when we have little more than our gratitude to offer him in return. It's just how he's wired and we are forever grateful that on our most recent trip to see him in Omaha he urged us to step it up and actually get this done. Shortly after that trip, we met Pia Nilsson and Lynn Marriot for dinner in Phoenix. Lynn and Pia authored the books that Matt and I compulsively highlighted and earmarked as junior golfers and young coaches. They echoed the encouragement provided by Sieck, provided the practical advice that we needed to get started, and then made a pivotal introduction to their friend, Matt Rudy.

Matt Rudy is the real reason you're holding this book in your hands. His experience, wisdom, and writing skills provided the direction and focus that we needed to organize our thoughts into something accessible and actionable to the everyday golfer. For over a year, we've traded emails, phone calls, revisions, and edits as he worked hard to help us reach our goal. He transformed many pages of long-winded and sometimes esoteric coach-speak into something legible and a final product that we are very proud of.

We also owe a debt of gratitude to the two legends that provided our forewords. Tim Lee is the godfather of motor learning research in golf. His works exposed us to another way of coaching and sparked a curiosity and an insatiable search for further education that has spurred our continuous improvement as coaches.

To just thank Cameron McCormick for his contribution to this book would be a great disservice to what he has meant to both Matt and me. He's provided an unbelievable model to follow as a husband, father, and friend. And there is no better coach in the world. Period. Don't take my word for it, just look at the results. No one works harder. No one cares more. No one approaches coaching with his level of sophistication and skill. Sometimes growing closer to someone you've looked up to and admired can be a disappointing experience. You find out they're actually human and maybe they don't do things all that different than you after all. The opposite is true for Cam. Every day I work alongside him my appreciation grows

for what he does and the standard of excellence he holds him and those around him to.

In addition to great mentors, Matt and I have been blessed with friends and family that offer unconditional love and support. One reward of finishing this project that I had not anticipated was being able to record my gratitude to these people in such a permanent medium. Special thanks to an awesome group of spectacularly-monikered friends—the Chain, the Wolfhogs, the Cuz, the Faz. To my Austin family; Wheels, Cobbler, Loukas, GG, ST, and the Bear.

Thanks to my sweet mother, an unlimited source of love and encouragement. Though she is a non-golfer and little in this book will resonate with her, she'll undoubtedly see it as a masterpiece. Also to my dad— who ignited my passion for golf and then inspired me to work as hard as I could. To Jeff, Rebekah, Dillon, and Katie—who continue to set the perfect example to follow. To Liz and Den for their always selfless support of our family.

To Oliver— for whom I hope the lessons in this book about learning and striving towards mastery will one day resonate with, regardless of the domain. Thank you to my wife and best friend, Kim. A beautiful, compassionate, and tireless superhuman charged with the impossible task of taking care of our family. Thank you for your limitless supply of support, love, and laughs—for reassuring when I'm doubtful, consoling when I fail, and celebrating even the smallest victories. I hope you'll be proud of this one.

—CL

SEPTEMBER 23RD, 2014 is a day that I will not forget. I was about 3 months into my role at La Rinconada Country Club, and Corey and I were out in Omaha, NE after a day with James Sieckmann, processing everything we learned that day. Inevitably, the topic of discussion shifted to thoughts of the future and how we were going to get to where we wanted to go. It was at that point where Corey suggested that I join him in his venture: Curious Coaches. It was an easy 'yes', and second only to my marriage, the best choice I've ever made.

Curious Coaches has evolved into more than just a blog. It has become an educational resource for coaches, has enabled us to share our message with our peers from around the world, and most importantly, an amazing partnership built on a respect and admiration, a healthy dose of competition, and a unrelenting desire for the other to be successful and fulfilled. So, thank you Corey for being you, inviting me to tag along and be a part of Curious Coaches, and most importantly, being a dear friend. As Amy Poehler and Tina Fey said best, "there's nothing better than making cool S*&% with your friends." I couldn't agree more.

So thank you, Matt Rudy, for translating our jargon and overly verbose prose into something unique. We hope this project stands to help motivated golfers around the world make real change and permanent progress. Your patience and expertise, and now friendship, are truly appreciated.

It is equally important to acknowledge the countless people who have challenged me to think differently and to strive towards continual improvement.

Starting with Cameron McCormick, who has been an amazing mentor and friend dating back to 2010. Your willingness to share your wisdom and insights is invaluable, and something I value deeply. Thank you for always challenging me to think critically about the way I do things.

To Henry Brunton, thank you for taking a chance on me and providing me with not only the opportunity to become a better coach, but also your continual guidance and support. The experience and expertise you have shared with me are foundational to my philosophy.

To James Sieckmann, Lynn Marriott and Pia Nilsson, and Derek Ingram thank you for continually sharing your insights and guidance. Your support means a lot!

To Mom and Dad, thank you for being outstanding role models, and for teaching me the value of hard work, education, and most importantly, never losing sight of your vision.

And lastly, to my wife. There's no other word to describe you other than amazing. Nothing that I've done could have done without your love and support. Thank you for your continued understanding and unwavering support of my need to leave no stone unturned in the pursuit of excellence.

—MW

RESOURCES

Now that you've read the book and experienced the practice plans, you may very well be interested in learning more about the philosophical and technical underpinnings of our ideas. To deepen your understanding of learning and performance, gain greater insights into the structure and sequence of the activities you just went through, and gain a more tangible perspective on the educational journey that has brought us to this point, we've compiled a list of some of the resources that have been most influential to us. As you'll see, they vary greatly—from golf books, to academic papers, and from science to philosophy. We hope you see fit to take the plunge and take a few steps long the path we are on.

Coaching & Learning
"Mastery" — George Leonard

"Developing Sport Expertise" — Dr. Joe Baker, Dr. Damian Farrow

"Flow: The Science of Optimal Experience"
— Dr. Mihaly Csikszentmihalyi

"Optimising Performance in Golf" — Patrick Thomas

"Conditions of Children's Talent Development in Sport"
— Dr. Jean Cote

"Reality is Broken" — Jane McGonigal

"Coaching Better Every Season" — Dr. Wade Gilbert

Golf Books

"Every Shot Must Have a Purpose" — Pia Nilsson, Lynn Marriott

"Play Your Best Golf Now" — Pia Nilsson, Lynn Marriott

"Your Short Game Solution" — James Sieckmann

"Your Putting Solution" — James Sieckmann

"Easier Said Than Done" — Dr. Rick Jensen

"Extraordinary Golf" — Fred Shoemaker

"Practice to Learn, Play to Win" — Dr. Mark Guadagnoli

Research Articles

Carson, H. J., Collins, D., & Richards, J. (2016). Initiating technical refinements in high-level golfers: Evidence for contradictory procedures. *European Journal of Sport Science*, 16(4), 473.

Chia, L. W., Keng, J. W. C., Ryan, R. M., & SpringerLINK ebooks — Education. (2015; 2016). *Building autonomous learners: Perspectives from research and practice using self-determination theory* (1st 2016 ed.). New York: Springer.

Guadagnoli, M. A., & Lee, T. D. (2004). Challenge point: A framework for conceptualizing the effects of various practice conditions in motor learning. *Journal of Motor Behavior*, 36(2), 212-224.

Schollhorn, W. (2012). The nonlinear nature of learning — A differential learning approach. *The Open Sports Sciences Journal*, 5(1), 100-112.

Porter, J. M., Landin, D., Hebert, E. P., & Baum, B. (2007). The effects of three levels of contextual interference on performance outcomes and movement patterns in golf skills. *International Journal of Sports Science and Coaching*, 2(3), 243-255.

Renshaw, I. (2012). Nonlinear pedagogy underpins intrinsic motivation in sports coaching. *The Open Sports Sciences Journal*, 5(1), 88-99.

Ryan, R. M., & Deci, E. L. (2000). Self-determination theory and the facilitation of intrinsic motivation, social development, and well-being. *American Psychologist*, 55(1), 68-78.

45759866R00080

Made in the USA
Middletown, DE
12 July 2017